THE
STERLING-DOLLAR-FRANC
TANGLE

THE MACMILLAN COMPANY
NEW YORK · BOSTON · CHICAGO · DALLAS
ATLANTA · SAN FRANCISCO

THE
STERLING–DOLLAR–
FRANC TANGLE

BY

PAUL EINZIG

NEW YORK
THE MACMILLAN COMPANY
1933

PRINTED IN THE UNITED STATES OF AMERICA
BY THE POLYGRAPHIC COMPANY OF AMERICA, N.Y.

To

NEGLEY FARSON

CONTENTS

vii

PREFACE

THE purpose of this book is to draw attention to the international aspects of monetary policy and to put the case for international co-operation in the monetary sphere. While it is a matter of general knowledge that the monetary policy pursued by any country produces effects far beyond its own borders, the international character of the whole monetary question has never been so forcibly in evidence as it has been during the last few years. It is now widely realized that the choice of the rate of stabilization for the franc—which was at the time considered a purely domestic affair—was largely responsible for the downfall of sterling and for the international crisis ; that the excessive depreciation of sterling was largely responsible for the accentuation of the downward trend of world prices ; and that the slump in the dollar and the uncertainties of its future course prevent the world from settling down to recovery, notwithstanding the fact that from a purely economic point of view the crisis has certainly passed its climax.

It was the lack of an international spirit in monetary policy that caused the failure of the Monetary and Economic Conference of June–July 1933. The author endeavours to show that the efforts to single out any one particular country, or group of countries, as being the villain of the piece, are futile. France, the United States, Great Britain and the other countries are all right from their own point of view in the monetary policy which they pursue and advocate. It is simply a misfortune that they have not been taught to try to understand the problems and difficulties of the other nations, and to adjust their national monetary policies to the requirements of international considerations.

Notwithstanding the failure of the Conference, the author refuses to share the gloomy views of those who prophesy the collapse of Western civilization. He firmly believes that the monetary deadlock will be solved, if not through an agreement then through the inevitable inflationary effect of the increasing economic difficulties. The choice lies between bringing about depreciation and devaluation by international co-ordinated action or allowing it to take its own course. The first alternative is to be preferred from every point of view, but even the last alternative would not mean the end of civilization.

While trying to understand the point of view of every country, the author ranges himself definitely on the side of those who approve the American policy of bringing about a considerable rise in prices by means of inflation. At the time of the suspension of the gold standard in the United States he sharply criticized the action of the new Administration because, with many others, he assumed that the object of the move was to compel Great Britain to stabilize sterling at the wrong time and at a wrong rate. In the meantime, however, he has had to realize that the suspension of the gold standard in the United States was just as inevitable as it was in Great Britain. It is true that sterling was swept off gold, while the suspension of the gold standard in the United States was a deliberate action. But, in deciding to take that fateful step, President Roosevelt merely accelerated the inevitable, for as a result of the unbearable burden of internal indebtedness the United States would have been driven off gold in any case sooner or later. So long as this excessive indebtedness is not liquidated through an adequate depreciation of the currency, there can be no stability either in the United States or in the rest of the world. In the author's opinion a policy aiming at a rise in American internal prices is an inevitable necessity; and the only possible way to agreement in the monetary field would be an adjustment of the currencies of other countries to the new level of the dollar.

P. E.

THE WHITE COTTAGE,
  SOUTH BOLTON GARDENS, S.W.
    August 1933.

THE STERLING-DOLLAR-FRANC TANGLE

CHAPTER I

INTRODUCTORY

IN a period rich in disappointments, the Economic Conference held in London in the summer of 1933 was the worst of them all. Admittedly, it was generally regarded as hopeless from the very outset. But nevertheless, most people, in their innermost hearts, really placed great hopes in it. They were, of course, reluctant to acknowledge this in public for fear of being regarded as incurable optimists : and they therefore left optimistic talk to those who, being in responsible positions, had perforce to profess their faith in the success of the Conference in order to justify the time and energy they spent in participating in it. But, from the very first week of the Conference, it was evident that the chances of even a partial success were very remote. The

Conference was on the verge of a complete break-down on countless occasions, and in the circumstances even the fact that it could carry on until the end of July, and that it adjourned peacefully instead of ending in a violent rupture, ought to be regarded as an achievement.

Every time the Conference threatened to arrive at a deadlock, there was an outburst of mutual recriminations ; the leading participants accused each other freely of being responsible for the breakdown, while the minor participants reproached the big ones for having invited them to London and then sent them home empty-handed simply because the leading powers could not come to an agreement between themselves.

From the first day of the Conference the United States was represented by Europe as the villain of the piece. For, was it not her government which, by deliberate policy, had caused the depreciation of the dollar just before the Conference and during its initial stages ? Was it not Washington's economic nationalism which made it impossible to come to an agreement on a provisional stabilization of the dollar during the Conference ? Was it not the rapid changes in President Roosevelt's policy that deprived the Conference of any fixed point on which it could depend ? Was it not the lack of authority of the American delegation, disowned by Washington on frequent occasions, that prevented the Conference from making some progress towards an agreement? All these accusations are unquestionably justified, but they represent only one side of the picture.

Those who accused the United States the most freely were themselves subject to a barrage of attacks. The Continental gold countries, which were at pains to represent the United States as responsible for the failure of the Conference, had themselves a good deal to account for. Was it not France and her associates who, by their stubborn insistence upon stabilizing the dollar, defeated their own object? Was it not they who were just as incapable of seeing the point of view of other countries as was the United States? Was it not this gold group which, out of sheer indignation at the tone and contents of President Roosevelt's famous " Independence Day " note, wanted to bring the Conference to an end at the beginning of July? Was it not they who, from that time onwards, concentrated all their efforts on preventing the Conference from discussing anything essential? All these accusations are just as solidly founded as those directed against the United States.

Nor did the British Government escape its due share of criticism. Was it not their irresolute foreign exchange policy, hesitating between the gold group and the dollar, that prevented matters from coming to a head in time for the Conference to be able to achieve some useful work ? Was it not the spineless attitude of Great Britain towards the question of monetary policy which was responsible for the failure to achieve at least a majority agreement to which the dissenting minor participants would eventually have had to submit ? Was it not the orthodoxy of the British attitude in the matter of public works that discouraged the Conference to a great extent ? All these charges are unquestionably justified.

All the other participants of the Conference have their own share in the blame. The only aim of Soviet Russia was to fish in troubled waters, and Germany, while thoroughly enjoying the fight between France and the United States, was primarily concerned with her own little game of debt repudiation. Every country, big or small, seemed to have come to London exclusively to get as much out of the Conference as it possibly could without itself intending to give anything at all.

From all this array of mutual recriminations it

is difficult to single out any one particular cause as chiefly responsible for the failure. If there is, however, one factor which stands out among the others, it is the extreme nationalism of the leading countries in the matter of currency policy. The Conference disclosed an amazing lack of understanding as to the international character of monetary problems. The belief that monetary policy is the private affair of every country reigned more than ever supreme. And it was this conception, more than anything else, that killed the Conference. Each of the three major participants, Great Britain, France and the United States, wanted to work out the world's salvation on the lines which suited its own conception of its individual national interests, without paying due regard to the national interests of the remaining countries. Already, before the Conference, two of them had declared that the discussion of fundamental problems of currency would have to be left outside the scope of the Conference. Each of the three expected the other two to regard its internal requirements with understanding, but failed to show any signs of similar understanding towards the internal requirements of the others. The United States expected France and Great Britain to realize the internal problems which made it necessary for her to suspend the gold standard and to adopt a policy aiming at the depreciation of the dollar. France expected the United States and Great Britain to understand why she regarded the stability of the franc as sacrosanct and beyond question. Great Britain expected France and the United States to understand the necessity for obtaining certain preliminary conditions without which it would not be safe to stabilize the pound. None of them was prepared to modify its viewpoint for the sake of an international understanding.

Admittedly, they could hardly be blamed for refusing to sacrifice national interests to international considerations. As we shall see in later chapters, the United States was perfectly justified in trying to work out her salvation through raising prices at all costs. France was perfectly justified in refusing to adopt a policy which might lead to a recurrence of the disastrous experience of 1924–6. Great Britain, in turn, was perfectly justified in refusing to repeat the error of 1925 by a precipitate stabilization of sterling at an unwarranted high level. But if this is so, why then summon a Monetary and Economic Conference, with the emphasis laid on the first part of the title ? The very nature of the Conference presumed that the principle of the international character of mone-

tary policy was admitted. In reality this was far
from being the case.

One of the lessons of the present crisis has been
to make the world realize the immense international
bearing of national monetary policies. In his
book, *The Tragedy of the Pound*, the author drew
attention to the backward state of the world's
thought in this respect. International Law, which
usually follows new developments fairly closely,
seems to have ignored completely, so far, the
international aspect of monetary policy. In *The
Tragedy of the Pound* the author drew a comparison
between the advanced state of International Law
regarding the respective national rights of two
nations bordering on the same river and its backward state regarding monetary policy. The various uses of a river are subject to detailed regulations
fixed by treaties, and century-old practice has
developed a set of definite rules in International
Law. The development of air transport within
the last decade or two was followed closely by the
development of rules regulating the international
problems arising from it. No sooner did the
invention of broadcasting conquer the ether than
International Law extended its scope to this new
sphere, regulating the international aspects of
broadcasting. It is only monetary policy which

has remained unchallenged as the national preserve of each individual country.

Before the war the international aspects of monetary policy were hardly recognizable. The gold standard worked automatically in the leading countries and the disturbance caused by the departure from it by some minor country was not sufficiently important to disturb the international atmosphere and to necessitate international action. And yet, in some instances the international character of monetary systems was recognized. The Scandinavian Monetary Union and the Latin Monetary Union bear witness to this. On the whole, however, the conception that monetary policy was the sovereign right of each state was taken for granted and was never questioned.

During the war the principal allies co-ordinated their monetary policies to some extent in the interests of the common cause. This arrangement was, however, discontinued soon after the armistice and the monetary policies of the countries concerned resumed their essentially national character. During the first few years that followed the war there could indeed be no question of any co-ordination. In most countries monetary policy in the real sense of the term did not exist, and the monetary situation was the passive result of a variety of factors, amongst which the budgetary situation played a prominent part. It was not until the beginning of the period of reconstruction that international influences began once more to make themselves felt in the monetary policies of some countries. The countries whose currencies were stabilized under the auspices of the League of Nations had to undertake to submit to the terms prescribed for them by the League authorities as to the guiding principles of their monetary system and of their future monetary policies. One of the main objects of the presence of foreign advisers in those countries was to see that the monetary policy of those countries should not depart from these principles. The monetary policy of Germany was to a great extent regulated by international agreements such as the Dawes Plan and the Young Plan. In all these instances the countries who were prepared to sacrifice in part their sovereignty in matters of monetary policy were the financially weak countries.

The question of attempting to bring the monetary policies of the stronger countries under international influences did not arise until later, well after the stabilization of sterling in 1925. Even as far as the financially weak countries were concerned, the level at which the currency was stabilized was usually decided upon by the governments themselves, without much regard to international considerations. Nor was there, as a matter of fact, any serious attempt to induce them to co-ordinate the rate of stabilization with any central plan, or even to take into account any established principles in fixing it. The only consideration which played an important part in the choice of the rate of stabilization was each country's desire to undervalue its currency sufficiently to be on the safe side. This principle unquestionably helped each individual country to work out its own salvation, but the result was that a considerable part of the world had its currencies undervalued in relation to those of the rest of the world. While the undervaluation of, say, the Austrian currency alone made but little difference from an international point of view, the undervaluation of the currencies of the greater part of central, eastern and western Europe became a factor of great importance in subsequent years.

The League of Nations, in arranging the reconstruction and stabilization of a number of currencies, proceeded in a haphazard way which has so far escaped criticism. On the surface the League authorities were admittedly systematic—in fact too systematic, as far as certain details were concerned.

Apparently, their aim was to make the currency and banking systems of all countries uniform. To that end they disregarded those individual circumstances which would have justified, and indeed really necessitated, differences between the systems of individual countries. They used all their immense moral and material influence in bullying small countries into accepting systems which did not suit them, and whose disadvantages gave rise subsequently to a great deal of trouble. The fact that most countries yielded to the pressure shows that it was an unrivalled opportunity for the co-ordination of monetary policies. The greater part of Europe was willing to submit to the conditions dictated by the League because of their desperate need of the League's assistance. But, in their use of this immense power, the League authorities mistook the shadow for the substance. They were gratified if all countries whose currencies they reconstructed agreed to adopt the same text for their central bank statutes, and did not attempt to use their power for more important ends. They would then have been easily in a position to establish the principle of internationalism in monetary policies. In the course of the arrangements for stabilization under their auspices, they could have elaborated fundamental principles as regards the international considerations which should guide the fixing of a new rate of stabilization.

It is true they had no direct influence over the strong countries, and they would not have been in a position to compel them to conform to those principles. Once the principles were established, however, there would have been strong moral pressure to induce the strong countries to adhere to them. To give only one example, we may recall that the gross undervaluation of the French franc, on the occasion of its legal stabilization in 1928, passed without a sound of protest abroad. In the following three years it became the source of immense international difficulties and was, in fact, mainly responsible for the collapse of the pound and for the whole world crisis. In the absence of any clear-cut ideas about the internationality of monetary policy, it was considered only natural, in 1928, that France should choose the level she liked for her own currency. Although during the period of pre-stabilization, which began at the end of 1926 and ended with the legal stabilization in 1928, it became evident that the franc was undervalued, it did not occur to anybody to raise the question of the international repercussions of the choice of the rate of stabilization. Had the League of Nations used its influence to force the principle of internationality of monetary policy upon the smaller nations, the world would by 1928 have realized the importance of the question, and it would have been aware that a unilateral decision on the part of a country of the importance of France was a violation of those principles. However, the League of Nations can hardly be much blamed for failing to think in 1924 in terms of the ideas of 1933.

Between 1927 and 1931 attempts were made to obtain the recognition of the international character of monetary policy. The attempts to establish close co-operation between central banks were in substance a struggle between the national and international viewpoints. The efforts of Great Britain to induce the other leading countries on a gold basis to co-ordinate their monetary policies were met with resistance in France, since she was pursuing a national monetary policy. To some extent the principle of internationality has been admitted in practice, as central banks have undertaken to renounce their rights to draw on the gold reserves of other central banks without their consent. On the whole, however, the attempt at co-operation failed to establish the principle of internationality. Nor did the establishment of the Bank for International Settlements achieve very much in that direction. It left the sovereignty of States in the matter of monetary policy intact, just as their political sovereignty was left intact by the establishment of the League of Nations.

Even the crisis of 1931 failed to make the world realize immediately the necessity of adopting the principle of internationality. In fact the collapse of the pound was a signal for the adoption of a *sauve qui peut* attitude by all the central banks. Individual depositors are often blamed for losing their heads and causing the failure of their otherwise solvent banks by the wholesale withdrawal of their deposits. But between 1931 and 1933 the world's central banks, which purport to represent the highest stage in financial wisdom, behaved in exactly the same way as ignorant and illiterate depositors do in times of panic. Each one was thinking only of its own deposit, little caring if the wholesale withdrawals to which they contributed undermined the stability of the dollar, or if they unnecessarily accentuated the weakness of the pound. This is a clear example of the disastrous results of the absence of international spirit in monetary policy. It was not until the failure of the Economic Conference that people began to take any serious notice of the problem at all. It became, however, evident by then that, when national monetary policies come into conflict with each other, the world is bound to suffer in consequence. It remains to be seen whether the realization of this is sufficiently general to secure the success of the second part of the Conference, if and when it is again convened.

There is, of course, no hope for the universal and complete adoption of the principle of internationality. So long as political frontiers exist, nations will always wish to retain their right to be masters of their own monetary policy. To expect that a strong independent country will ever submit its monetary policy unconditionally to some international authority is as optimistic as to expect the universal adoption of complete free trade. So long as politically the world is not merged into one great unit the nations will always reserve the right to raise tariffs against each other and to direct their monetary policies according to their own requirements. In the past, however, every nation has on occasion been willing to relinquish temporarily, for a definite period or subject to a certain notice, its sovereign right to impose duties on the goods of other nations. Every trade treaty is based on this sort of partial and provisional abandonment of national sovereignty in the matter of tariffs and other commercial questions. And it may, therefore, well be asked whether it is too much to expect the same system to be extended to monetary policy also. Any attempt to abolish the national character of monetary policy is doomed to failure, but to attempt to bring about compromises similar to those involved in trade treaties is perhaps not a hopeless task.

CHAPTER II

NATIONAL ASPECTS OF MONETARY
POLICY

THE sovereignty of the State in the matter of
monetary policy has not hitherto been called in
question. Nor is it the object of the present book
to do so. While stress is laid upon the international aspects of monetary policy, it will be
emphasized that national aspects should be duly
taken into account. They are of the utmost importance, and must be borne firmly in mind by
anyone advocating progress towards a higher
degree of internationality. The object of the present
chapter is to indicate the principle reasons why
monetary policy has always been essentially national,
and why it is always likely largely to remain so.

Among the many means at the disposal of the
State to promote the welfare of its citizens, monetary policy occupies a leading position. To say
that it is the most important means of Govern-
mental influence would be an exaggeration. What-

ever the results of monetary policy may be, they do not approach in importance the results of the State's decisions concerning war and peace. Apart from this, however, monetary policy ranks second to none of the other prerogatives of the modern State. Without minimizing the economic, political and social consequences of fiscal policy or commercial policy, for instance, we may say that the results of monetary policy overshadow them. It is only in countries with a managed economic system, such as Soviet Russia and, in a much smaller degree, Italy, that economic policy overshadows monetary policy in its effects. By bringing about a rise or a fall in prices, by making monetary resources scarce or plentiful, by making the price of money high or low, the State is in a position to affect the welfare of every one of its inhabitants. It can give them—temporarily at any rate—the appearance of prosperity, or it can plunge them into poverty and ruin. It can encourage an expansion of production and consumption, but it can also force producers to reduce their output and consumers to cut down their requirements. It can encourage the commercial utilization of new inventions, and can also induce a reduction of output costs by enforcing rigid economies. It can turn its nationals into spendthrifts, but it can also make them extremely thrifty. All this can be achieved by the simple means of causing a rise or a fall in prices.

This is, however, by no means everything. The very social structure of the State can be altered through monetary policy. The Government is in a position to strengthen the rentier classes or to wipe them out. It is in a position to relieve the debtor classes of the burden of their debts or to increase this burden beyond the limit of their capacity. It can strengthen the working classes, middle classes, or the " upper ten ", or it can reduce any one of them to poverty. It can virtually confiscate property and it can create entirely new wealthy classes. From a political point of view, it can strengthen the position of the ruling classes or parties and can weaken the opposition or the oppressed classes.

Is it surprising that the nations are unwilling to let this immense power, or even a part of it, pass into foreign hands ? If they were to agree to have their taxation system, or their customs tariff, determined by an international body, they would be admitting much less foreign influence in their vital national affairs than they would by consenting to international regulation in matters of monetary policy.

There is, however, an even more important reason why the State cannot relinquish its sovereignty in the matter of monetary policy. To put it briefly, monetary policy is to a great extent independent of the will of Governments. The State is virtually omnipotent in determining the nature of taxation or tariffs, but in the sphere of monetary policy it is often a helpless victim of circumstances. For instance, it is useless for a Government to decide to deflate, or even to maintain the stability of its currency, if its budget shows a huge deficit which can only be covered with the aid of the printing press. Even if Governments were willing to submit their monetary policy to international ruling, circumstances might arise from time to time which would prove more powerful than either national or international decisions. The case of inflation caused by a budgetary deficit is one example. In certain circumstances, it is impossible for a Government to cut its expenditure or to increase its revenue sufficiently to wipe out the deficit ; nor is it possible, except temporarily, to finance the deficit with the aid of non-inflationary methods. Another characteristic instance, showing that Governments are not always masters in their own houses as far as monetary policy is concerned, is provided by British Bank rate policy

between 1925 and 1931. Had the British authorities followed the time-honoured orthodox rules,
they would have kept the Bank rate high for some
time so as to bring about an adjustment of home
prices to world market prices.   Instead, the political
pressure arising through the existence of over a
million unemployed compelled them to keep the
Bank rate at the lowest possible figure even at
the risk of losing gold through an outflow of funds.
In face of pressure of this kind, it is difficult to
imagine any Government deciding to follow an
international policy which is in conflict with the
national requirements of the moment.

The volume of currency and credit is a further
factor which does not always depend on the will
of the authorities.   It is often influenced by forces
against which the Governments and central banks
are powerless.   Nor do the rates of exchange obey
arbitrary dictation.   The Government is not always
in a position to bring about a radical improvement in the trade balance, and, if the weakness
of the exchange is due to a deficit in the balance
of trade, no international undertaking can compel
the Government to prevent a depreciation of the
national currency.

Nothing but the adoption of an international
currency would make it possible always to adopt

the monetary policy directed by international agreement. The volume of currency would then be regulated by agreement ; although even under these conditions the volume of credit would be subject to national influences, for the same amount of currency would not serve as a basis for different amounts of credit in various countries. Ruling out the Utopian idea of the adoption of an international currency, we must resign ourselves to the fact that monetary policy is and remains essentially national. The national character of the monetary policy is more pronounced in times of crisis than in relatively normal periods. Even before the present crisis, however, it came to the fore from time to time. For instance, the strong opposition of the Middle West to New York's Bank rate policy ever since the end of the war was a characteristic manifestation of monetary nationalism. Again, the refusal of the French authorities to relieve the pressure on London by lowering their Bank rate in 1930 shows the strength of national interests as against international requirements. During the present crisis the national character of monetary policies has become only too painfully evident. The monetary policy of the leading countries has been characterized by an utter disregard of international considerations.

If nationalism reigns supreme in current monetary policy, it is much more the case as regards momentous decisions affecting the monetary system. Anything that is done, or is left undone, in the course of the management of the current monetary policy, is usually capable of being remedied if necessary. When it comes, however, to decisions such as the determination of the rate of stabilization, then the responsibility of the authorities concerned becomes much graver. If they are not prepared to yield to international considerations in the conduct of their current monetary policy, they are much less likely to do so in deciding on changes in the monetary unit or in the monetary system. Such decisions are, indeed, anything but easy even if they depend upon purely national considerations. The struggle between conflicting interests in France before the stabilization of the franc clearly showed the difficulties confronting any Government in choosing a rate of stabilization. Whatever rate is chosen is bound to antagonize large sections of the population. The position of Governments confronted with such dilemmas is anything but enviable. They have to sacrifice the interests of part of the nation in order to serve the interests of the rest. How much more difficult their position would be if, in addition to domestic

considerations, they had to take into account the
legitimate wishes of other countries ! It is always
difficult enough to pacify the interests adversely
affected by the decision on the grounds of its being
necessary for the sake of general national interests.
But to persuade the victims of the decision that
they had to be sacrificed for the sake of international considerations would be a well-nigh
hopeless task. The argument that in the long
run there is no difference between national and
international interests sounds most unconvincing
to anyone who is called upon to pay the price for
the internationalism of a Government's monetary
policy. While the advantages of national policy
are usually direct and obvious, those of an international policy are usually indirect and difficult
to ascertain. Let us take an example illustrating
the case. The undervaluation of a currency is in
accordance with the immediate interests of exporters and producers. If those interests outweigh
those of rentiers and people with fixed incomes, then
the undervaluation of the currency may be said
to be in accordance with the national interests.
In spite of this, the Government of a country
may be induced by international considerations to
abstain from undervaluing a currency so as to
avoid the international repercussions of such an

act. It would be extremely difficult, however, to convince exporters that, taking a long view, it is to their interest to forgo the advantages of an undervalued currency.

And yet it is the duty of Governments to face such difficulties. Without trying to underestimate the powerful influences tending to emphasize the national character of monetary policy, we propose to show in the next chapter that situations may arise where international considerations should outweigh considerations of national interest in the narrower sense of the term.

CHAPTER III

INTERNATIONAL ASPECTS OF
MONETARY POLICY

In the previous chapter we enumerated the arguments in favour of a national monetary policy. Let us try now to examine the arguments in favour of an international policy, so as to be able to form an idea of their relative importance. We pointed out in the last chapter the immense influence of monetary policy upon a nation's welfare. It is now our task to indicate the immense influence of the monetary policy of a country beyond its own frontiers. The countries which we are concerned with at present are, of course, only those which are of great importance from a financial point of view. The influence of the monetary policy of smaller economic units is only considerable if it provides an example which is followed by other nations.

In the first place, we shall confine ourselves to the international aspects of current monetary policy. The primary weapons with which policy is made effective are changes in the Bank rate. The international effects of such changes are too well known to require detailed examination. A Bank rate change can only be effective if it exerts influence outside the country concerned. If a central bank raises its Bank rate in order to attract funds from abroad, those funds will have to come from somewhere. The influx to country A must necessarily be the efflux from country B. And a movement which tends to strengthen the currency of A is bound, therefore, to weaken the currency of B. Moreover, the rise in interest rates brought about in country A is not likely to confine itself within its boundaries. Owing to the existence of innumerable financial links, the rising tendency will tend to spread over other countries. Thus, an act of the monetary authorities of country A affects the monetary situation of countries B, C, and D, which were no party to the original act. In practice, a rise in the Bank rate in one country of importance is usually followed by a wave of Bank rate increases all over the world. This may occasionally be due to international influences which affect all countries alike. On other occasions, however, it is the monetary policy of the country initially concerned which originates the international tendency.

While the international effect of Bank rate policy is a matter of general knowledge, the international effect of policies of monetary expansion or contraction is not so generally recognized. In theory, a rise or fall in prices caused by an expansion or contraction of credit should confine itself to the country concerned, and the only international repercussion should be a depreciation of its exchange. In practice, however, things do not always work out that way. Very often the rise or fall in prices in an important country results in a sympathetic movement of prices abroad. This means that the monetary policy of country A is capable of influencing prices in country B. And the population of the latter may have a justifiable grievance against the former for causing their prices to move in an unwanted direction. If country B is also a big country it may have the satisfaction of knowing that on other occasions it is country A that suffers in the same way through the monetary policy of country B. The economically weaker nations have not even this dubious satisfaction. They have to put up with the influence of the stronger countries without ever being able to reciprocate it.

Hitherto we have only been considering the external effects of national monetary policy brought

about involuntarily by the authorities of the countries concerned in the course of pursuing what
they considered to be national interests.   On occasion, however, Governments have been known to
go deliberately out of their way to influence the
monetary policy of a foreign country.   The most
typical of such cases during recent years was the
action of the French in 1927, when they deliberately caused a contraction of the monetary resources of London.   At that time France was suffering from an acute *embarras de richesse* as a result
of the heavy inflow of funds through the repatriation of French balances from abroad and through
foreign speculation on a rise of the franc.   In order
to prevent this double influence from resulting in
an unwanted appreciation of the franc, the French
authorities had to undertake to buy all the foreign
currencies offered in excess of the requirements of
the market.   The result was an expansion of the
note circulation which threatened to cause a rise
in prices.   To avoid this, the French authorities
set themselves the task of discouraging the buying
pressure on the franc.   They had no means of
preventing the repatriation of French balances—
in fact, it was to their interest that the process
should continue—but they made an attempt to
check bull speculation in francs.   This bull specu-

lation was financed largely out of the liquid resources of the London market, which were created
largely through the accumulation of official French
sterling balances.   In order to reduce the amount
of these floating funds, the Bank of France under-
took the withdrawal of some millions of pounds
of gold from the Bank of England.   It was the
declared object of these transactions to deplete
the monetary resources of London.   This was, however, contrary to British monetary policy, which
aimed at easy credit conditions.

It is not often that the monetary authorities of a
country adopt the course of deliberately working
against another country.   In a way it would be better
if there were more such obvious cases of deliberate
interference with another country's monetary policy,
for it would bring home the necessity for international agreements.   As it is, it is doubtful whether
public opinion in general is capable of properly
realizing the necessity for such agreements.   The
conclusion of peace treaties has to be preceded by
the waging of wars, and it is possible that the conclusion of monetary treaties will have to come as
the final act of a currency war.   There has been
much talk about the possibility of such developments, but so far the currency war has remained
a threat voiced by leader writers.   Although we

have several examples of one-sided interference with another country's monetary policy, there has not been, so far, any obvious case of a deliberate clash between the monetary policies of two countries through measures directed against each other. The sphere in which such a clash may occur is that of foreign exchange policy. Should, for instance, the British authorities attempt to cause a deliberate appreciation of the dollar by buying it in the open market, and should at the same time the American authorities aim at deliberately bringing about an appreciation of sterling in the same way, we should be confronted with a case of open currency war. Whatever might be the outcome of such developments, it would certainly strengthen the case in favour of the regulation of monetary policy by international agreements. Disastrous as such a currency war would be in its immediate results, it might prove to be " the war to end war ".

Without actually taking the extreme course of attacking each other in the sphere of monetary policy, the Governments of various countries can do immense harm to each other through a depreciation race. Until the present crisis, the idea of such a policy was almost entirely unknown. During the period of post-war currency chaos the depreciation of various currencies was not the result of any deliberate policy aiming at out-bidding other countries in that direction. It is a matter for heated discussion whether or not the depreciation of the mark was wholly or partly deliberate, but in any case, even if it were so, it did not aim at out-bidding any other country. The only countries besides Germany whose currencies depreciated to an extent comparable to the depreciation of the mark, were Soviet Russia, Poland, Austria and Hungary. None of these countries was a commercial rival of Germany, and the depreciation of the mark was certainly not engineered in order to out-bid that of either the rouble or the krone. Nor was there any sign of rivalry in the sense of a depreciation race between the countries whose currencies depreciated to a relatively moderate extent only. On the contrary, most Governments endeavoured to keep the depreciation as moderate as possible. Thus the Italian Government stabilized the lira at too high a level, while Great Britain and the Scandinavian countries went so far as to restore their currencies to pre-war parity. The nearest thing to a depreciation race was the decision of the French and Belgian Governments to devalue their currencies to a greater extent than was strictly necessary. In the case of the Belgian currency, this was a *bona fide* mistake, for the Government did not allow itself any time for testing the rate chosen for stabilization.   In the case of the French franc, however, the undervaluation was deliberate.

It was the immense success of the French policy which may be regarded as being responsible for sowing the seeds of depreciation racing.   The undervaluation of the franc became the source of immense financial strength and economic prosperity.   The Bank of France succeeded in accumulating the largest gold reserve possessed by any country per head of population.   French producers and merchants benefited by the undervaluation of the franc both at home and in foreign markets.   The economic crisis seemed to have left France unaffected until 1931, and even then she only began to feel its full weight after the slump in sterling.   Financially, the undervaluation of the franc made France into a first-class power whose influence was felt all over the world.   Nor did she suffer morally through the deliberate undervaluation of the franc.   Notwithstanding the fact that the value of the franc was reduced by four-fifths, and that millions of investors, French and foreign, suffered considerable losses thereby, confidence in the franc and in the French Government's credit returned almost

immediately after this act of default. Although
sterling was restored to its pre-war parity, from 1928
onwards the franc enjoyed more confidence than
sterling. By 1930 the French Government's credit
stood at 4 per cent against the British Government's
5 per cent.

Faced by these facts, it is impossible to avoid
the conclusion that the memory of the public is very
short and that the merits or demerits of Governments and their currencies are judged, not by their
past records, but by their present position. It is
true that the strength of the franc and of the French
Government's credit was due to default, but this
did not alter the fact that they were strong. It is
equally true that the weakness of sterling was due
to excessive honesty in returning to the old par,
but this again did not alter the fact that it was
weak.

Had the French monetary policy resulted in
collapse and disaster, nobody would have been
tempted to follow its example. In fact, the example
of Germany acted as a deterrent against any temp-
tation to yield to pressure in favour of reckless
inflation or currency depreciation. The example
of France proved, however, that if inflation is
checked at a relatively moderate stage a country
can enjoy all its benefits without having to bear

the full burden of its disadvantages, which manifest themselves only at a more advanced stage. The success of the French devaluation must have converted an immense number of people all over the world, consciously or sub-consciously, in favour of moderate inflation and undervaluation of currencies.

This mentality was in no way responsible for the suspension of the gold standard in Great Britain, which was a matter not of choice but necessity. Once the deed was done, however, the French example must have influenced British public opinion to no slight extent in favour of avoiding any repetition of the mistake of overvaluing the pound, all the more so as British experience appeared to be confirming the inferences drawn from the previous experience of France. In Great Britain, as in France, the undervaluation of the currency resulted in an improvement in the trade balance ; it brought about a restoration of confidence in the currency ; it brought into active use immense wealth which was previously either hoarded in the form of gold or deposited abroad ; it increased the country's influence in the sphere of international finance. But for these glaring facts, the orthodoxy of the British authorities and of academic quarters might have outweighed the forces favouring a prolonged instability of the pound, and sterling would probably have been stabilized long since at a too high level. As it is, most people saw no reason why this country should not benefit, in exactly the same way as France had before, through an undervaluation of sterling.

It was inevitable that the French example, thus confirmed and reinforced by the events in Britain, should be followed also by other countries. Japan was the first country to follow in Great Britain's footsteps. After a vain effort to maintain the gold standard, she allowed the yen to depreciate to an extent well in excess of the depreciation of sterling. The result was decidedly favourable to Japanese interests. It brought about a rise in internal prices, which created a certain degree of prosperity in the home trade, and Japanese foreign trade also benefited by the depreciated exchange in so far as it was not counteracted by higher tariffs, political boycotts, and other restrictions. Denmark was another country to follow the British example. After having maintained the kroner for a while at par with sterling, the Government yielded to the pressure of exporting interests and allowed it to depreciate from about 19 to about 22½. At the time of writing, new pressure is being brought to bear upon the Danish authorities to induce them to allow a further depreciation to a rate of 30 to the pound.

It was not, however, until the suspension of the gold standard by the United States that the world began to become conscious of the meaning of a depreciation race. Although the purpose of allowing the dollar to depreciate is undoubtedly mainly concerned with the internal situation, this would not prevent the development of a depreciation race with other currencies. Up to the moment, Great Britain has not taken up the challenge implied in the depreciation of the dollar by the deliberate policy of the United States Government. In face of the slump of the dollar, sterling was maintained stable in relation to gold currencies at the cost of heavy sacrifices. The question is, however, how long can this continue. Until 1931, France only enjoyed the advantages of the depreciation race without its inconveniences. It was only when Great Britain's turn came to outbid her in the depreciation of her currency that she began to feel the adverse effects. Similarly, between September 1931 and April 1933 Great Britain had all the advantages of the depreciation race without much of its inconvenience. It is true that she suffered through the Japanese competition caused by the depreciation of the yen, but on balance she was

decidedly the principal beneficiary of the " race ".
From April 1933 onwards she had to cede this
privilege to the United States. It is now the latter's
turn to reap the benefits of outbidding the other
major countries in the depreciation competition.

It is now evident that the advantages obtained
from a depreciation race can last only until some
other country depreciates its currency to a greater
extent. In a community where everybody is honest
a dishonest individual has all the advantages of not
being handicapped by moral considerations. If,
however, his fellow human beings become just as unscrupulous as he is then he will have no more advantages than any honest individual has in an honest
community. In fact, he may come to the conclusion
that dishonesty is not worth while. This is exactly
how the participants in a currency depreciation
race are liable to feel about it after they have been
defeated with their own weapons. They might
come to the conclusion that it is worth their while
to renounce any prizes that might accrue from the
depreciation race so long as they are safeguarded
against being defeated in it.

Thus, the depreciation race is likely in the end to
lead to a victory for the international conception of monetary policy. So long as there is only
one country which uses poison gas, no moral

considerations would ever induce it to relinquish the use of that weapon. If, however, its use is open to all potential belligerents, they may be inclined to consider the idea of coming to an agreement to outlaw that weapon. Similarly, the weapon of currency depreciation will become less attractive if every country which is tempted to use it runs the risk that some other country may use it more extensively. The fear of being defeated in a currency depreciating race, or of winning a victory in circumstances which are almost as bad as defeat, may induce the Governments to be a little less obsequious to the dictates of the purely national aspects of monetary policy.

CHAPTER IV

THE DEPRECIATION OF STERLING

PARADOXICAL as it may sound, situations may arise—and have in fact arisen more than once in financial history—in which the weakness of a currency becomes the strength of the country concerned. The German exchange dumping of 1920-3 still lives in the memory of our generation to prove what a source of trouble a depreciating currency can become to other countries. At one time, in the relatively early stages of German inflation, it was, in fact, believed that Germany might be able to avenge herself upon her oppressors by ruining their trade with the aid of exchange dumping. Fortunately for us, the rapidity of the process of depreciation prevented Germany from taking full advantage of the weakness of her currency. France provides another characteristic example of the strength of a country being founded upon the weakness of its money. In fact, her case proves that the advan-

40

tages may even outlive the period of weakness.
For although the depreciation of the franc came
to an end in 1926, France continued to enjoy
the benefits of an undervalued currency until
five years later.

In 1931 it was the turn of Great Britain
to benefit by the weakness of her currency. Up
till that time she had dissipated a good deal of her
energies and resources in keeping up an appearance of strength. For six years sterling resisted
the powerful undercurrents threatening to undermine its stability. In September 1931 the fight had
to be abandoned for lack of ammunition. With
the resources for the defence of sterling exhausted
to the last cent, Great Britain had to acknowledge
her weakness in the monetary field openly by
allowing sterling to depreciate. The moment the
fiction of strength was discarded and the reality
of weakness was acknowledged, Great Britain's
situation underwent a complete change. In the
economic sphere, the menacing growth of un-
employment came to an end, and a moderate
tendency to revival set in. At the same time,
the unsound situation of the trade balance began
to correct itself, and Great Britain made some
progress towards a greater degree of self-sufficiency. In the sphere of finance, the Government

succeeded in balancing the budget, and before long it was in a position to solve the extremely difficult problem of War Loan conversion. In the political sphere, the period of instability was followed by one of the most stable periods since the war. Even from a moral point of view the depreciation of sterling was the signal for a complete change. Before September 1931 the British nation was becoming more and more demoralized, but the shock administered by the depreciation of sterling brought forth the finest qualities inherent in the national character. In the international field, Great Britain was once more in a position to make herself felt as an active and powerful factor, instead of being at the mercy of those who were in a position to support or frustrate her efforts to keep sterling stable.

It would be difficult, of course, to prove the direct relation of cause and effect between all these changes and the depreciation of sterling. There can be no doubt about it, however, that, had Great Britain attempted to continue by some means to defend the stability of sterling, none of these welcome developments would have been seen.

Within a few months from the suspension of the gold standard the weakness of the pound sterling had become the source of immense power. From a vulnerable currency exposed to the caprices of speculation, sterling developed, in fact, into something like a world dictator. Never in the past, when the stability of sterling was above suspicion, had that currency possessed such immense influence over economic and financial tendencies all over the world. In order to understand this spectacular change it is necessary to give a brief summary of the evolution of sterling after September 1931.

The immediate result of the suspension of the gold standard was a depreciation of sterling to its natural level. Everybody agrees that when in 1925 sterling was raised to its old parity of 4·86, it became hopelessly overvalued. By removing the artificial barriers of gold points, sterling was allowed to find its true level. It is difficult, however, to induce the pendulum to stop immediately when it has reached its point of equilibrium. From being overvalued sterling went to the other extreme and became undervalued almost immediately after the suspension of the gold standard. This is only natural, for it is the characteristic of market mentality to believe in the lasting nature of the tendency of the moment, whether in an upward or downward direction.

The effect of the undervaluation of sterling upon world price levels was immense. It shared with the gold withdrawals from the United States the responsibility for the accentuation of the falling trend of commodity prices. This was due in part to the fact that, since Great Britain is the principal buyer and consumer of many commodities, the decline of her external purchasing power through the depreciation of the pound sterling was bound to affect the world's commodity markets. This effect was all the stronger because in a period of depression it is buyers rather than sellers who determine prices. Another factor of equal importance was the depreciation of the currency of a number of producing countries in sympathy with sterling. The currencies of the greater part of the British Empire, and those of a number of other countries, followed the movements of sterling to some extent, and their exporters were thus in a position to undersell the producing countries on a gold basis. The latter, in order not to lose their markets, were compelled to adjust their prices to a great extent to those prevailing in the so-called sterling group.

Towards the turn of the year, the pendulum began to swing back. The undervaluation of sterling resulted in tendencies to correct the anomaly. Throughout the first quarter of 1932 sterling had a strong rising tendency, which the British authorities were unable completely to check. The rising trend continued to a more moderate extent also during the second quarter of the year. Its result was a recovery in world prices which began to make itself felt during the third quarter and which was accompanied by a general feeling of optimism. It was believed during the third quarter of 1932 that the end of the crisis was at last reached, and that we were on the way to recovery.

Unfortunately, these hopeful feelings proved to be short-lived. The second half of 1932 witnessed a gradual depreciation of sterling which became accentuated towards the end of the year. The result was an all-round relapse in world prices, which began to move towards new low records. History repeated itself, however, and after the turn of the year the sterling pendulum began to move once more in an upward direction. It would have moved a good deal higher and a good deal faster, but for the more or less successful efforts of the British authorities to check it. These efforts were a target for heated criticism abroad, and Great Britain was accused of being responsible for the immense difficulties brought about by the continued fall of prices. Indeed, as we have seen above, it would be idle to deny the direct influence of the movements of sterling upon the world price level. There can be no doubt that the depreciation of sterling was one of the most important contributory factors responsible for the fall in prices, and that a reversal of the movement would have been able to bring about a noteworthy recovery.

But, in spite of this, it is hardly fair to blame the British authorities for having failed to manipulate sterling in the way that would have best suited the interests of the gold countries. Events had proved more than once that it was impossible to maintain sterling at a high level. On three occasions, in October 1931, during July–December 1932, and from April 1933 onwards, the appreciation of sterling in terms of gold currencies was inevitably followed by a relapse. This clearly proved that the British authorities were not in a position to raise sterling to a higher level and maintain it there for any length of time. In the circumstances it was a wise policy to aim at preventing an excessive rise in sterling, so as to avoid, or minimize, the disturbing effect of unnecessary fluctuations. This was the aim pursued by the Exchange Equalization Fund, and, although the details of its working are open to criticism, on the whole it may be said to have largely attained its end.

Great Britain has been accused of having secured internal economic stability, and a moderate degree of relative prosperity, at the expense of the rest of the world. This accusation would be well founded if the depreciation of sterling had been the result of a deliberate policy. This was, however, by no means the case. Ever since the suspension of the gold standard the British authorities have adhered to the view that sterling should be stabilized at the highest possible level at which it would stand a chance of being maintained. In the early days, the Treasury had a rate of 4 dollars in mind, and it was only with great reluctance that, under the pressure of facts, it revised this figure later in a downward direction. The depreciation of sterling took place, not in accordance with the wishes of the Treasury, but in spite of its policy. It is true that this country derived considerable advantages from the depreciation. These advantages were not, however, obtained as a result of deliberate policy ; they were a windfall, for which nobody in particular can be praised or blamed, whichever may be the appropriate way of looking at it.

Apart from its effect upon the internal position, the depreciation of sterling has strengthened the influence of Great Britain in the international sphere. While in August and September 1931 she was constrained to humiliate herself by asking for support from France and the United States, and had to submit to their terms, in the spring of 1932, and again in the spring of 1933, she became a supreme arbitrator over the fate of other currencies. It was the support provided by British buying of dollars that saved the dollar in 1932 ; it was our decision to withhold this support by pegging sterling to the franc that sealed the fate of the dollar in 1933. The granting of a credit of £30,000,000 to France was largely responsible for the strengthening of the franc. The periodical flight of capital towards London has placed that centre in an exceptionally strong position to help or to withhold assistance according to circumstances. The accumulation of large foreign balances and gold resources through the working of the Exchange Equalization Account has, moreover, increased the active power of Great Britain beyond the actual amounts involved.

It is true that during the first half of 1932, and again during the first quarter of 1933, the British authorities concentrated their energies upon preventing a rise of sterling. But for the intervention of the Exchange Equalization Fund, sterling would have appreciated considerably on both occasions. This would have deprived Great Britain of a large part of the advantages gained by the depreciation of sterling, and, at the same time, it might have provided some degree of relief to the gold countries in the form of a recovery of world prices. In spite of this, it is unfair to accuse Great Britain of having pursued a selfish policy with complete disregard of interests other than her own. Admittedly she benefited by the policy pursued, but this was not the main reason she pursued it. Had there been a fair chance of maintaining sterling at the level to which it might have appreciated but for the intervention of the Exchange Equalization Fund, most probably our authorities would not have hesitated to sacrifice immediate national advantages for the sake of an international recovery. As things were, however, it was only too obvious that there was not the least chance of sterling being maintained at such a height. The favourable tendency was on both occasions plainly of a temporary nature. It did not arise from any considerable improvement of the trade balance, nor from any permanent inflow of capital. Although there was some improve-

E

ment in the trade balance after the suspension of the gold standard, it was not nearly sufficient to account for the rising tendency of sterling on either occasion.

As for the inflow of foreign capital which took place early in 1932, and again early in 1933, it was evidently of a temporary character. The movement was due to the transfer of restless international liquid funds which, for the past two years or so, had been moving from one centre to another, causing inconvenience by their arrival and frequently spelling disaster by their departure. By far the greater part of the inflow of funds consisted of these utterly undependable balances—rightly termed " bad money "—which are here to-day and may be anywhere to-morrow. To build upon such an elusive factor would have been entirely unjustifiable. It is true that the result of the inflow was an accumulation of the resources available for the defence of sterling. As, however, the counterpart of these resources was represented by a corresponding amount of sight liabilities to foreign countries, subject to withdrawal for the slightest reason, it could hardly have served as a basis for stabilization. Admittedly the technical situation was the same as this before we went off the gold standard, and even before the war, when London's stability was beyond question. But, in the light of the experience of recent years, it has become evident that in the changed conditions such a basis for the stability of sterling would be highly inadequate. Amidst the uncertainty created by the events of the last few years, which are likely to live in the memory of the public for some time after the restoration of stability, it has become necessary to possess a solid surplus of liquid assets over and above international short-term liabilities. As the British authorities possessed no such surplus, either in 1932 or in 1933, they were fully justified in distrusting the apparent firmness of sterling. They were right in resisting this rise as far as they could. Had they allowed sterling to take its natural course, it would have appreciated very considerably, much to the disadvantage of British interests. Even the benefit which other countries might have derived from such an appreciation of sterling would have been essentially temporary, and the resultant rise in world prices would have been followed by a sharp relapse which would quite probably have accentuated the crisis further.

It has often been stated that the British Government intended to make use of the power conferred upon it by the depreciation of sterling for bargaining purposes. Great Britain was suspected of trying to secure advantages in the commercial field, as well as in the matter of war debts, by the skilful handling of the foreign exchange situation. As far as the commercial advantages were concerned, they were a natural consequence of the depreciation of sterling. But, in fact, Great Britain was to a very great extent prevented from obtaining the full commercial benefit of the depreciation. The moment sterling left its gold basis a number of countries took defensive measures in the form of additional customs duties, quotas, exchange restrictions, etc. In the circumstances, the extent to which foreign exchange policy could be used to secure commercial advantages was limited. Conceivably the possibility of a further depreciation of sterling may have been helpful in the Trade Treaty negotiations, but this factor should not be overrated. What really mattered in this respect was the fact that Great Britain had bought more from foreign countries than she had sold abroad, and, once she became conscious of this fact, it placed her in an exceptionally strong bargaining position even without any support from foreign exchange policy.

As for the use of foreign exchange policy as a bargaining weapon in the matter of the British war debts to the United States, the fact is that on repeated occasions members of the British Government stated in public that there could be no question of stabilization until, amongst other things, the problem of war debts was settled. This has been construed in some quarters as an attempt to bring pressure to bear upon the United States to be more accommodating with regard to the debts. In reality, the necessity for regarding the solution of such an important problem as a preliminary condition of stabilization appears to be perfectly natural. The mere statement of such an obvious truth, that there could be no stabilization without war debts settlement, could hardly be regarded as an attempt at political blackmail. It would have been, indeed, very poor financial statesmanship to attempt to stabilize sterling while the question of war debts was still an uncertain factor. Even if the aim of these statements was to influence the American attitude towards war debts settlement, this aim was fully justified, not merely from a British, but also from an international point of view. The stubbornness with which the United States insisted upon her strict dues has been one of the main causes of all our economic difficulties, and any means, fair or foul, would have been fully justified if this stubborn attitude could thereby have been broken.

The accusation that the depreciation of sterling during the last quarter of 1932 was deliberately engineered to bring pressure to bear upon the United States is entirely unfounded. It is one thing to refuse to stabilize pending the settlement of war debts, and another thing deliberately to bring about the depreciation of sterling, with all its adverse effects upon the United States. The British Government may have been guilty of the first " offence ", but certainly not of the second. There was, indeed, no need for artificially staging a depreciation of sterling. Conditions were sufficiently adverse in themselves to do everything in that way. The British Government could not have been blamed if it had simply stepped aside and allowed natural forces to take their course. What actually happened was that, for some time, the Exchange Equalization Fund went out of its way to prevent a depreciation of sterling. Throughout September and during part of October, it was depleting its resources in an attempt to prevent a fall of sterling. It was not until the resources of the Exchange Equalization Fund declined to a low level that these efforts were abandoned. There was no need for any

intervention to exaggerate the adverse effect of
the war debt payment of December 15, 1932,
upon sterling. If the United States suffered
through the depreciation of sterling, she had only
herself to blame for it. Sterling depreciated, not
because of any action taken by the British Government, but in spite of all preventive efforts, as a
direct result of the uncompromising attitude of
the United States in the matter of war debts.

A great deal of publicity has been given to the
fact that, by choice or by necessity, a number of
currencies more or less followed sterling. Ever
since the suspension of the gold standard by Great
Britain there has been much talk about the " sterling bloc ", but few people have taken the trouble
to analyse its meaning. It is supposed to have
included the British Empire, the greater part of
northern Europe, and a number of countries in
other parts of the world. In reality there has
never been such a thing as a sterling bloc. From
a legal point of view there has never been any
agreement between Great Britain and other
countries for maintaining any fixed ratio between
their currencies, nor even any understanding for
maintaining their currencies approximately stable
in relation to sterling. Even the understanding
between the countries of the Empire was vague.

It is true that in the absence of agreements there was an unmistakable tendency for a number of currencies to move in sympathy with sterling. Those currencies, however, had their individual movements independently of sterling, just as the moon has its individual movement around the earth, apart altogether from its movement in connection with the solar system. Every now and again some member of the so-called sterling bloc decided either to break away or at least radically to change the relation between its currency and sterling. When in 1931 sterling was depreciating fast, at one time the Portuguese Government decided to prevent the escudo from following it any further. Again, in 1933, when sterling was rising gradually in spite of resistance by the British authorities, the Swedish Government considered it inexpedient that the crown should follow sterling indefinitely in its upward course. Again, in 1932, yielding to the pressure of Danish exporters, the Danish Government agreed to allow the crown to depreciate to 22·50 from its then rate of 19. Even within the Empire there were no fixed relations between sterling and other Imperial currencies. The Canadian dollar fluctuated somewhere half-way between sterling and the dollar, changing its allegiance from time to time. Until the end of 1932 the South African pound remained on a gold basis ; while the Australian pound remained remarkably stable at a 25 per cent discount, the New Zealand pound underwent a drastic adjustment in 1932. It may be said without exaggeration that there was hardly one member of the so-called sterling bloc which remained consistently faithful to sterling.

The suspicions that Great Britain was attempting to create a broader sphere of influence from which gold countries would be excluded were entirely unfounded. For a number of reasons, financial and commercial, many currencies had to follow sterling to some extent. There was, however, no actual deliberate effort on the part of the British Government to increase the so-called sterling bloc by inducing countries to abandon the gold standard. Whenever an English newspaper expressed pessimistic views about the prospects of a gold currency, a wave of indignation swept over the foreign Press, and the British Government was freely accused of engineering a Press campaign in order to undermine confidence in the currency in question. Those who are aware of the independence of the British Press from Government influence must realize the absurdity of such charges. At various Press conferences in Whitehall, which have become rather

frequent during the last few years, the spokesman of
official quarters expressed certain views on certain
matters, but no real attempt was made to force
them upon the Press by moral pressure. It is
simply unthinkable that any British newspaper
should receive official instructions to attack one
or another gold currency. In fact it was not
to the interest of the British Government to bring
about the suspension of the gold standard in other
countries. There was every reason to believe that
the advantages of the depreciation of sterling
would come to an end if too many countries followed our example. It would have been unwise,
for example, to deprive the British rubber industry
of the benefit of a low sterling rate by driving
Holland off the gold standard. Nor would the
British steel industry have much reason to be
thankful if the Government were to assist Belgian
or German steel exporters by causing the depreciation of their currencies. The outburst of
indignation with which the British Press and
public opinion received the suspension of the
gold standard in the United States gives some
indication of British sentiments on the subject.

It has often been stated that the British
authorities have been guilty of unnecessarily pro-
longing the period of international instability by

refusing to stabilize sterling. About this more will be said in a later chapter. Here let it be sufficient to point out that at no time since the suspension of the gold standard have conditions been suitable for the stabilization of sterling on a solid basis.

All this is not meant, however, to acquit the British Government of the charges of having pursued a selfish national monetary policy. Having been victimized by the selfish monetary and commercial policies pursued by other nations, Great Britain has undoubtedly departed to some extent from the traditional unselfish and internationally-minded attitude which, in the past, has proved to be highly advantageous even from a strictly business point of view. Circumstances were such, however, that there was no choice for her but to pursue the course which, taking a short view, may have appeared selfish. She had to suspend the gold standard because she was driven off it. She had to remain off gold because there was no chance for her to return to it. She had to maintain sterling undervalued in order to avoid harmful and unnecessary fluctuations. If she did take advantage of her situation, other nations in her place would have done so to a far greater extent.

CHAPTER V

THE CRISIS OF THE DOLLAR

THE collapse of the dollar in April 1933 took the world completely by surprise. The number of those who could claim to have seen it coming was incomparably smaller than that of the prophets who had foretold the fall of sterling in 1931. It is true that from time to time since October 1931 there had been spasmodic flights from the dollar, but this was not due to any definite anticipation of its collapse. Most of those holders of dollars who transferred their funds were, in fact, convinced that the odds were at least ten to one on the gold standard being maintained. Times were such, however, that few people cared to take even this fractional risk.

The conditions under which the dollar and sterling respectively collapsed differed in almost every respect. The same result was brought about by totally different sets of causes. There was, however, some similarity between the symptoms

which preceded their fall. During the period
between 1929 and 1931 sterling was subject to
repeated spells of selling pressure, as a result of
which it often depreciated to the vicinity of gold
export point, and remained there for prolonged
periods. The dollar underwent the same experience during the period 1931 to 1933. Until the
suspension of the gold standard in Great Britain
nobody thought of suspecting the dollar's stability.
Within a week of the fateful September 21, 1931,
however, signs of a flight from the dollar became
noticeable. This first attack was resisted without much difficulty. But, during the following
months, the weak trend renewed itself several
times, and on at least one occasion the American
authorities themselves were beginning to become
anxious about the danger of a collapse. From
October 1931 until the middle of 1932 the United
States was losing gold heavily and persistently.
This was largely, if not exclusively, the result of
the withdrawal of foreign balances. Where the
situation differed fundamentally from that of
Great Britain previous to the suspension of the
gold standard, was that the United States could
technically well afford to lose gold. From time
to time various figures were published announcing
the amount of " free gold " which the United

States was in a position to lose without having
to modify the minimum reserve ratio. These
figures varied according to the way they were
calculated, and the more gold that was lost the
larger was the figure which was stated to be available. In any case, it was well known that the
United States could easily pay off all the foreign
balances out of her surplus gold. From a technical point of view the only potential danger was
a wholesale flight of American capital. In reality,
however, the extent to which American capital
took flight abroad was, throughout the critical
period, relatively moderate. The American public is not used to investing abroad, and the
disastrous experience with foreign lending after
the war did not exactly encourage it to do so.
Conditions were so uncertain in every part of
the world that most Americans preferred to take
the chance of a depreciation of the dollar rather
than run the risk of losing their money abroad.
In any case, pessimism regarding the prospects
of the dollar was much less pronounced in the
United States than abroad. The mere idea that
the United States could ever suspend the gold
standard was regarded by most Americans as an
insult to the nation.

And yet, the heavy outflow of gold caused by

the withdrawal of foreign balances did not fail to produce a strong psychological effect in the United States. It was not the danger of a collapse of the dollar that was feared, but the repercussions upon the internal situation. The American public is easily influenced, and turns. panicky at the slightest provocation. The conception gained ground that in some vague way the decline in the gold reserve of the Federal Reserve system might interfere with the stability of the banks, and might endanger the security of deposits. It was feared that, should the drain continue, it might easily lead to a run on the banks. While technically the position of the dollar was unassailable, psychologically the selling pressure was none the less a source of danger.

During the second half of 1932, the dollar reaped the full benefit of the partial and temporary economic recovery which followed the improvement in sterling. The selling pressure eased and the outflow of gold came to an end. In fact, the Federal Reserve system was able to recover a large part of the gold lost during the first half of the year. It appears that in their anxiety to liquidate their reserves, various European countries went so far as to leave themselves without adequate dollar balances for current seasonal requirements. As a result, the autumn demand for dollars was accompanied by a flow of gold from Europe and the other continents to the United States. It seemed as if the danger was definitely over. President Hoover himself regarded it as a matter of past history, and on this assumption he made public reference, during the electoral campaign, to the narrow escape which the dollar had had in the previous spring. This was the first occasion on which it was officially admitted that there was at one time a danger of suspension of the gold standard. Had President Hoover not been convinced that the currency crisis was definitely over, he would never have dared to make such an admission in public. It was one of the biggest blunders made during the crisis. Many people remembered that at the time referred to by President Hoover's remark, official quarters were as emphatic as ever in their denials of any danger whatsoever. President Hoover's admission went a long way, therefore, towards discrediting the authorities in the eyes of the public. When, some months later, the dollar once more became vulnerable, no official reassuring statement was able to restore confidence.

Towards the close of the year the firm tendency of the dollar became accentuated. To some extent this was due to a flight from the franc, about which more will be said in a later chapter. The main reason for its firmness was, however, the anticipation of war debt payments. Throughout November the dollar appreciated in terms of sterling not merely on account of the anticipation of British and other European buying of dollars for war debt payments, but also owing to the psychological effect of this factor upon sterling. The more obstinate the American Government, Congress and public opinion showed itself in the matter of war debts, the more it became evident that the stabilization of sterling was out of the question. At the end of November, the sterling-dollar rate touched a new low record at 3·14.

Strange as it may sound, it was the firmness of the dollar which proved to be the source of its weakness a few weeks later. As a result of the psychological undervaluation of sterling, there was a fair scope created for its recovery as soon as the question of war debt payment was out of the way. The recovery of sterling actually began even before the payment was made, on the strength of the announcement that the payment would be made in gold, instead of by buying dollars in the open market. Towards the end of December, and especially in January, the

F

seasonal factor also began to turn in favour of sterling, and the knowledge that the tide had turned brought out a powerful bull movement. It was evident that sterling was undervalued, and business men all over the world hastened to cover their requirements well in advance. Apart from this, foreign balances which had deserted London during the second half of 1932 began to return there once more. The movement was all the more powerful as the British authorities prevented it from producing its full effect upon the exchange rates. Had sterling been allowed to take care of itself, it would have probably risen to 3·80 or 4·00 within a few weeks. As, however, the operations of the Exchange Equalization Fund kept it down for months, allowing it only gradually to rise to about 3·45, it remained attractive to buy. The bull movement assumed largely the form of buying sterling against dollars, and sterling's meat proved therefore to be the dollar's poison. American capital began to flow from New York to London, and the efflux of gold was resumed. But for the excessive depreciation of sterling through the war debt payment of December 15, this adverse pressure on the dollar early in 1933 would not have arisen. There is a suggestion of the hand of Nemesis in the fact that the shortsightedness of the United States in the matter of war debts recoiled upon the dollar.

It would be idle, however, to pretend that the dollar was the victim of merely technical circumstances which, despite its inherent strength, inevitably brought about its collapse. The truth is that the dollar was doomed in any case, not for international, but for domestic reasons. The real shock which caused its collapse originated internally.

In January 1933 the Senate decided that the list of the loans granted by the Reconstruction Finance Corporation should be made public. Seldom has any Parliament made itself responsible for such a deliberate act of mischief against the welfare of its country. Whatever the motives of this fateful decision were, they could not possibly justify an act which was bound to have a strong demoralizing effect. Everybody knew that the resources of the Reconstruction Finance Corporation had been drawn upon extensively by banks and other companies, but when the full list of the loans granted in support of these institutions were published—it ran to several closely printed pages—it brought home to the public the enormous extent to which American finance and industry needed assistance. The

publication of such a list would have been sufficient even in normal times to create panic. As
it was, it was published in a moment of extreme
nervous tension and produced, therefore, a maxi-
mum effect. Millions of American depositors
reached the conclusion that there was practically
no bank in the United States which they could
trust implicitly. The result was a run on the
banks of a magnitude which was without precedent even in the history of American banking
crises. The run began in Detroit for reasons
which appeared to be purely local ; but it had,
after all, to begin somewhere, and one motive
was as good as another to play the part of the
last straw. Before long the panic spread over
a number of states, and towards the end of
February and the beginning of March all states
had to declare some form of moratorium, partial
or complete, on the repayment of deposits.

Such a wholesale default could not fail to
influence the international position of the dollar.
The adverse pressure which had persisted since
the beginning of the year assumed sweeping
dimensions. Gold left the country in huge con-
signments, but even this was unable to allay the
selling pressure on the dollar. The situation
was much graver than a year before because on

this occasion the dollar was not supported by British official buying. While early in 1932 the British authorities pursued the policy of pegging sterling in relation to the currency which was subject to attacks, later they completely reversed this policy. Towards the end of 1932 they adopted the practice of pegging sterling in relation to the stronger of the gold currencies. When the rising trend of sterling was mainly due to a flight from the franc, the Exchange Equalization Fund sought to counteract it by buying dollars. When the buying pressure came through the weakness of the dollar, the Exchange Equalization Fund prevented an appreciation by pegging sterling to the franc.

Thus, during the critical weeks of February and March there was no British buying to offset the selling pressure on the dollar. The reasons for this change of tactics on the part of the British authorities are manifold. They are dealt with in detail in the author's book *The Comedy of the Pound*. Here let it be sufficient to say that when abandoning the dollar to its fate there was no desire whatever on the part of the British authorities to see it fall ; in fact, they had nothing to gain and everything to lose through the suspension of the gold standard in the United States.

They could hardly be expected, however, to assume responsibility for bolstering up the dollar against such an immense pressure. Their task was to prevent an unwanted rise in sterling, and this could be achieved without having to take the risk of acquiring huge dollar balances. It will be remembered that, when sterling was subject to a similar attack in 1931, the terms under which the United States was prepared to assist us to a limited extent were hardly generous. The credit granted in support of sterling had to be in terms of dollars ; it bore a very high rate of interest and it was practically secured on the Bank of England's gold reserve. It would, indeed, have been too much to expect us to support the dollar in a way which left the full exchange risk on our shoulders without yielding us any interest except the low rates prevailing in the short money market in New York.

In spite of its violence, it was not the international attack on the dollar that brought about its fall, except in so far as it aggravated the internal situation. But the outflow of gold was accompanied by internal hoarding on a gigantic scale. The gravity of the banking situation increased day after day. Hoarding of notes assumed unprecedented dimensions, in addition to the hoarding of gold. The situation was rapidly becoming unbearable.

On his assuming office in March 1933, President Roosevelt made a desperate attempt to save the stability of the dollar by declaring a general banking moratorium and an embargo on gold withdrawals. This method had proved to be successful in Germany, as it saved the stability of the Reichsmark during the crisis of 1931. It was hoped that the result would be the same in the United States. It was assumed that the so-called " bank holiday ", and other measures, might check the pressure on the banks and would thus remove the main source of danger. Those who are inclined to criticize President Roosevelt's measures of March 1933 should remember that his position was extremely difficult. He had to take over the responsibility of Government in the middle of a grave crisis which required immediate action. He had no time to consider what to do, but had to act first and think afterwards. As the obvious symptoms of the panic were the withdrawal of gold and the run on the banks, the measure which lent itself most obviously to his purpose was to stop gold withdrawals and the withdrawal of deposits. In theory, the United States could have well afforded to continue to pay out gold. In practice, however, any further losses of gold would have accentuated the internal panic, and this had to be prevented at all costs.

A question which has been subject to much discussion, but which is of purely academic interest, is whether the gold standard in the United States was suspended on March 4 or on April 19. Strictly speaking, the moment a country imposes an embargo on gold exports it ceases to be on the gold standard. If it suspends the convertibility of its notes internally, this is also in itself sufficient to disqualify it from claiming to be on a gold basis. In addition to having done both of these things, the United States went still further by taking steps to recover the gold withdrawn internally during the weeks of panic which had preceded the imposition of the embargo. And yet many people claimed at the time that the United States was still on a gold basis after March 4. In the light of post-war experience the conception of the real nature of the gold standard has become rather vague. From a broad point of view, any country whose currency is maintained stable in relation to gold may be regarded as being on a gold basis. And, as the dollar maintained its stability until April 19, it

is not altogether unreasonable to accept the contention of those who took the view that the March
measures did not constitute an actual suspension
of the gold standard.

There appeared to be no reason, indeed, why
the suspension of the convertibility of notes and
the embargo on gold export should result in a
depreciation of the dollar. After all, the trade
balance of the United States was still favourable,
though less so than a year before. In addition,
she was still receiving payments from many of
her foreign debtors. It was therefore only natural
that when, after a week's bank holiday, the foreign
exchange market reopened, the dollar was quoted
in the vicinity of the rate at which it was quoted
before the bank holiday. During the weeks that
followed, it did not require any special efforts
to keep the dollar from depreciating. From an
international point of view there should have
been no difficulty whatsoever in maintaining the
dollar at par in spite of the virtual suspension
of the gold standard in March.

In the circumstances, the deliberate decision of
the United States administration to go off gold
definitely in April took the world completely by
surprise. It came like a bolt from the blue to
the foreign exchange markets. It was not due

to any selling pressure on the dollar, through speculation or through the withdrawal of foreign or American capital. The author's view is definitely that the United States authorities deliberately engineered a minor run on the dollar so as to have an excuse for abandoning the gold standard.

On the Thursday preceding Good Friday the market in dollars was remarkably uneventful in Europe throughout the day. In London, foreign exchange dealers were inactive and most of them took advantage of the lack of business to leave for the holiday in the afternoon. Suddenly, after 5 p.m. when there was hardly anybody left in the London foreign exchange market, comparatively heavy selling of the dollar began to be noticeable from New York. In half an hour the sterling-dollar rate was up several points and the movement continued while London and the European markets were closed. Next day, when most continental markets, together with London, remained closed, the selling pressure went on, and the dollar declined below gold export point in relation to the French franc. The volume of transactions was negligible and, had the American authorities desired to maintain the dollar, they could have done so at a trifling cost. There was, however, no sign of support ; in fact, there is

every reason to believe that the selling occurred
with the knowledge and approval of the American
authorities. At that time the banks were terrified
of President Roosevelt, and would not have dared
to defy him by acting against his wishes. For
this reason it is difficult to believe that the selling pressure was due to a mere leakage of information about the decision to go off gold. It
seems much more probable that, having decided
to take that step, the American authorities had
to stage, for the sake of appearances, an attack
on the dollar which would, to some extent, conceal
the deliberate character of the suspension. Otherwise, the fall of the dollar would have been too
reminiscent of an over-insured ship which is capable of sinking in the calmest sea.

Once the run was initiated, there was no need
for any further effort to accentuate it. It will
be remembered that in the case of sterling the
fact that on various occasions the exchange was
allowed to decline below gold point was mainly
responsible for undermining confidence. It is not
surprising, therefore, that the depreciation of the
dollar below gold point during the holidays should
have aroused a similar wave of pessimism. During the two days that followed the opening of
the European markets after Easter Monday, the

dollar was subject to heavy selling pressure. Even then it would have been possible, at the cost of 50 to 60 million dollars of gold, to stop the run. Instead of this, the American authorities cancelled the arrangements already made for gold shipments, and on April 19 it was officially announced that the United States was no longer on a gold basis.

This deliberate act of " walking off " the gold standard caused immense indignation abroad. It was the first time in history that a nation had suspended the gold standard without having been obviously forced to do so by circumstances. From a moral point of view this step appeared to most people unpardonable. It has done more than any other event in modern history to undermine confidence, and at the first moment it appeared as if it were the death blow to the gold standard system itself. Up till that time the public always had some indication and warning when a country was about to suspend the gold standard. The depletion of its gold reserves in itself provided dependable evidence. The case of the United States proved, however, that it is possible for a country to go off the gold standard even if it has the largest gold reserve in the world. After such an experience the public could hardly be blamed if it ceased to trust the stability of even the best-secured currencies. There is no doubt that the United States broke her pledge to pay out gold in spite of the fact that she possessed ample gold for that purpose.

The indignation was particularly strong in this country, because the decision was generally regarded over here as a diplomatic move on the part of the United States to secure a better bargaining position in the forthcoming Economic Conference. Until then Great Britain, as the only leading country off the gold standard, held all the trumps. Although the British Government disclaimed any intention of using the question of stabilization as a negotiating counter at the Economic Conference, it was hoped none the less that the importance of this factor would play an important part in bringing about a compromise. Now, all of a sudden, while Mr. MacDonald and the British delegation were on their way to the United States to conduct preliminary negotiations, the Washington administration confronted them with a *fait accompli* by going off the gold standard. This act brought about a complete reversal of the respective bargaining positions of Great Britain and the United States. With the dollar depreciating, the bargaining position of the United States became much stronger, as she had a good deal more to concede and a good deal less to ask. It was generally believed that the main object of the suspension was to create this situation. The United States authorities and the Press were largely responsible for this impression, as during the first twenty-four hours they did not fail triumphantly to point out the change. It was only on the second day that it occurred to them to furnish the explanation that their decision was entirely due to the internal position. Even then they had to be very guarded in their explanations. It was simply unthinkable that they should have to confess that they were driven to the suspension of the gold standard by the fact that 99 per cent of American banks were to all intents and purposes insolvent, unless and until revolutionary measures were taken to raise commodity and share prices.

CHAPTER VI

AFTER THE COLLAPSE

THE suspension of the gold standard in the United States was a staggering blow, and yet the world has taken it much better than at first appeared likely. The international effect of the slump in the dollar was not nearly as harmful as that of the slump in sterling two years earlier. The suspension of the gold standard by Great Britain was followed by a long series of suspensions elsewhere ; and it was expected that the depreciation of the dollar would have a similar effect. Actually, however, up to the time of writing, Estonia is the only country which has followed the American example. This is perhaps because, between 1931 and 1933, most weak countries had already suspended the gold standard or had made arrangements to maintain it in a modified form. The strong countries, on the other hand, have displayed a much more stubborn resistance to the influence of the American example than was anticipated.

While the collapse of the pound was followed by a serious crisis in various parts of the world, the fall of the dollar had no such consequences. Possibly this was because, in the meantime, the crisis had spent most of its force ; most of the weak elements had been eliminated by failure or by assistance ; and commodity and security prices had touched rock-bottom. In such circumstances the world was in a better position to stand such a shock than it had been two years earlier.

Over and above all, the beneficial effect of the change upon the internal position in the United States could not but affect the international situation favourably. The suspension of the gold standard has removed that intolerable atmosphere of suspense which was largely responsible for the American internal crisis of 1933. It will be remembered with what a sigh of relief the British public took the suspension of the gold standard in 1931. The same thing occurred in the United States in 1933, only on a much more exaggerated scale. The great majority of the American public had, indeed, more obvious reasons than the British public to be pleased about it. The advantages liable to accrue to Great Britain from the enforced suspension of the gold standard were very abstract, and, beyond a vague feeling

that a change was bound to work out for the better,
very few people could explain the reasons for their
satisfaction.   In the case of the United States the
suspension affected the immediate personal interests
of the majority of the public.

We stated in a previous chapter that the United
States Government was driven to its decision by
the fact that 99 per cent of the American banks
were to all intents and purposes insolvent.   This
was the result of the fall in commodity prices,
which had made the major part of mortgage loans
hopelessly frozen.   As the value of rural and urban
real property dropped to a fraction of its boom
level, and became to a large extent unsaleable, it
was evidently hopeless to expect any payment
until a rise in the price level took place.   The
frozen mortgages of the banks, together with their
loans on securities, which were inadequately
covered, had rendered them completely insolvent,
and the instinct of the depositors in claiming their
funds back was therefore perfectly understandable.
Their simultaneous action, however, brought matters to a head, when the situation might otherwise have been tided over until the banks had
recovered their position.   Confronted with the
wholesale withdrawal of deposits, which was not
altogether checked even by the drastic measures

of March 1933, the Government had three alterna-
tives. It could allow nature to take its course,
which would have meant the failure of most of
the banks and general ruin all over the country.
It could have assumed responsibility either for
mortgages or for bank deposits, which would have
meant practically doubling the amount of the
public debt overnight. The third course was to
take extreme measures to bring about a rise in
commodity prices. Had either the first or the
second course been applied, the public would
have had to pay in one form or another the full
price for it. The suspension of the gold standard
made possible, however, a solution by which the
taxpayer stood to lose relatively little. It was
decidedly the easiest and most popular course to
choose. To some extent debtors received direct
relief from the Government, but this and other
measures were the only means to the main objective of raising prices.

The immense number of debtors in the United
States had every reason to rejoice over this solution.
It is true that, in theory, the debtors' advantage
is bound to be paid for by the creditors. In practice, however, the creditors were well aware that
they had nothing to gain and a good deal to lose
by any attempt at a solution on the basis of the

price level existing in April 1933. Insistence on
full payment on that basis would have meant
wholesale default ; Government guarantee would
have meant increased taxation, the burden of
which would have fallen back upon the creditors'
shoulders. All they could hope for was some meagre
compromise by which debtors would be enabled
to discharge part of their liabilities according to
their capacity. The depreciation of the dollar, if
carried sufficiently far, would enable the majority
of debtors to pay in full. It is true that to receive
payment in depreciated currency means a loss to
the creditor, but it is a much less painful operation
than any arrangement by which he would not get
the same amount of dollars as he lent.

The American public as a whole was therefore
justified in welcoming the change. Nor was their
optimism damped by any feeling of uncertainty
lest the movement might get out of control. In
this respect the situation in the United States in
1933 compared very favourably with that of Great
Britain in 1931. The United States had all the
gold she needed and was in a position to call a
halt at any moment. The American public had
the assurance that the depreciation of the dollar,
which was engineered deliberately, would remain
under the control of the authorities. This initial

optimism on the part of the public went a long way towards bringing about the much-needed rise in commodity and security prices.

It was generally expected that the suspension of the gold standard would not be followed by any marked depreciation of the dollar. Taking all material factors into consideration, there was, indeed, no reason why the dollar should depreciate at all. As we have previously pointed out, the trade balance was still favourable, and many of the foreign debtors of the United States were still paying. Although the price level was higher than in Great Britain, it was more or less in equilibrium with those of the gold countries. Experience in the past has shown that, whenever economists base their conclusions upon material factors without allowing sufficiently for psychological influences, they invariably prove to be wrong. In the case of the South African pound, for instance, most experts agreed, at the time of the suspension of the gold standard, that there was no reason whatever for it to depreciate to par with the pound sterling ; and yet before many weeks the premium on the South African pound had disappeared. In the case of the dollar, it was again the psychological factor which, in defiance of the material factors, resulted in an early depreciation of about 15 per cent. The speculative anticipation of rising prices and dollar depreciation more than counteracted all the favourable material factors. Before very long the sterling-dollar rate exceeded the landmark of 4·00, a rate which even a few weeks earlier was considered in England as simply unthinkable.

The effect of the fall in the dollar upon the position of the gold currencies was much less pronounced than was anticipated. In fact, some people maintain that the crisis of the dollar actually saved the franc. As a result of the huge budgetary deficit and the French Government's efforts to meet it through increased taxation, the stability of the franc was threatened by a flight of French capital. This flight assumed menacing proportions in December 1932 and January 1933. In spite of the strong technical position of the Bank of France it might have led to the suspension of the gold standard. The crisis of the dollar, however, diverted attention from the franc, and, as the storm centre shifted from France to the United States, the breathing space thus obtained enabled the French Government to improve the budgetary situation and the Treasury's cash position. Moreover, as the depreciation of the dollar had the appearance in the early stages of being directed against Great Britain, it resulted in a Franco-British *rapprochement*, the first fruit of which was the conclusion of a French credit of £30,000,000 in London. Although from time to time there was a run on the franc and on the other gold currencies, they were well able to withstand it.

The immediate result of the suspension of the gold standard in the United States was a sharp rise in the price of raw materials and food products. The rise in these prices was much more rapid and more pronounced than the depreciation of the dollar exchange. In this respect the situation was developing in a totally different way from that experienced by other countries with depreciated currencies. It is a commonplace of post-war books on currency that the exchange is the most sensitive of all financial barometers. When a currency depreciates, the tendency manifests itself in the first place in an adverse exchange movement. The next stage is a rise in the wholesale price of staple products which again is followed by a rise in the wholesale price of other commodities. It is only in the later stages that retail prices and other items in the cost of living begin to rise. The experience of the United States in 1933 departed altogether from this schedule, and the wholesale prices of certain commodities easily outdistanced the exchange rate in registering the depreciation

of the currency. The reason for this peculiar
phenomenon lay primarily in the fact that Americans were not anxious to invest their capital abroad.
In Germany, France and Great Britain, fear of the
depreciation of the national currency induced a
number of people to export their capital. It is
this flight of capital which accentuates the depreciation of the exchange disproportionately to the rise
in commodity prices. In the United States the
flight of capital abroad was relatively moderate.
Although the exchange control was far from water-
tight, the extent to which the public took advantage
of its many loopholes was not very large. While
anxious to safeguard their capital against the depreciation of the dollar, Americans were unwilling to
take the risk involved in sending it abroad. Instead, they preferred to buy either equities or commodities. The latter has become quite a popular
form of investment even for small capitalists. In
the United States it is by no means unusual for
clerks to own a few tons of tin, or a number of
bales of cotton. Thus, while the demand for
foreign currencies was relatively smaller than in
other countries with inflationary experience, the
demand for certain commodities was much larger.
This explains sufficiently why such commodities
were rising more rapidly than the foreign exchanges.

Thanks to this unusual phenomenon the world benefited by the depreciation of the dollar to an unexpected degree. We have seen that, when sterling was depreciating, its effect was a fall in world market prices. The depreciation of the dollar produced exactly the opposite effect. Internal prices of commodities with a good international market rose more rapidly than the exchange value of the dollar depreciated ; by the working of the laws of simple arithmetic, the result was inevitably a rise in commodity prices abroad. Being the largest producing country in the world, the United States occupies a special position in the international economic system ; and she carried sufficient weight to impose her prices upon the world market. Admittedly this was so because a rise in prices was more than overdue. However it may be, the depreciation of the dollar proved to be a blessing in disguise. Those responsible for it meant to sacrifice international interests to American interests. But, much to their own surprise, they rendered a valuable service to the rest of the world.

It has taken the world a long time, however, to realize this. For weeks and months after the suspension the United States was subject to hostile criticism. Every fresh depreciation of the dollar

was followed by a fresh outburst of indignation,
and it was regarded as a deliberate act of sabotage.
The anti-American outcry attained its height
when the United States Government announced its
decision to disregard the " gold clause " (i.e., the
promise to pay principal and interest of its debt
" in gold coins of the United States of the present
weight and fineness "), and to pass legislation enabling other debtors to follow its example. Whatever view we may take as to the moral aspects of
the act—it certainly amounted to a cold-blooded
repudiation which would more than justify the
European Governments discontinuing the payment
of their war debt to the United States—it was an
inevitable consequence of the same causes which
were responsible for the suspension of the gold
standard. As most long-term debts in the United
States had a gold clause, the depreciation of the
dollar would have provided no relief to them if the
validity of the gold clause had been upheld. Nobody with any practical sense can blame the United
States for facing realities and sacrificing a principle
which, in the changed circumstances, had become
untenable. The sooner it is realized that mankind cannot be victimized for ever by the rigid
maintenance of *status quo* and the inviolability of
vested interests, the better for everybody concerned.

CHAPTER VII

DEFENCE OF THE GOLD CURRENCIES

AFTER following the destinies of sterling and the
dollar during the critical years 1931 to 1933, let
us turn our attention now to the Continental gold
currencies. The French franc is by far the strongest
and most important of these. Notwithstanding
this, it has never, since 1931, been completely above
suspicion. The weak point in the defences of the
French franc has all along been the budgetary
situation. Apart from this the position in France is
decidedly sounder than it was in the case of either
Great Britain or the United States. Although
foreign balances have been transferred in moderate
amounts to Paris, their amount has never been
sufficiently large to constitute in itself a potential
danger to the franc. Nor is the internal debt situation unfavourable. The factors, therefore, which
forced Great Britain off the gold standard, and
which made the United States decide to go off it,
are absent in the case of France. On the other

hand, a situation might arise in which the budgetary situation might render the franc vulnerable, notwithstanding the technical strength of the monetary position.

When, after having saved the franc, Monsieur Poincaré retired from active politics, he left France with a balanced budget and with a huge Treasury surplus. Indeed, France was suffering from an *embarras de richesse* because of the immobilization of her money market resources through the accumulation of this Treasury surplus. Under M. Poincaré's successors, however, this surplus quickly dwindled down to nothing, and the budgetary surplus gave way to large and increasing deficits. In such circumstances the Government was unable to follow the British example and effect a substantial reduction in the burden of the public debt through conversion operations. It is true that a large conversion was carried out towards the end of 1932, but the net saving achieved thereby was not sufficient to make a material difference to the budgetary situation. Throughout 1932 the Treasury had to call upon the leading banks to provide the funds required for meeting the current deficit. Very much against their will, the banks had from time to time to take over large blocks of Treasury Bills. In doing so, they were constrained to impair their liquidity to a very considerable extent. It was obvious that before long all the available liquid resources of the commercial banks would be exhausted, and the Treasury would then have to call upon the resources of the Bank of France, which would have meant inflation. The anticipation of this possibility was largely responsible for the existence, notwithstanding the huge gold reserve, of pessimism regarding the future of the franc.

There was, however, another reason for taking a gloomy view of the franc's prospects. In their efforts to cover the deficit, the Governments which had followed each other in close succession had attempted to increase taxation. The Frenchman's dislike for paying taxes is proverbial, and the aggravation of the economic crisis was not likely to change his feelings. The moment there was serious talk of increasing taxation, the flight of French capital abroad became accentuated. When the Radical-Socialist Government sought in 1932 to prevent this flight by draconian measures, the result was only a further accentuation of the movement in anticipation of stricter measures. It was this flight from taxation rather than any flight from the franc owing to a distrust in its stability which caused the selling pressure on the French exchange in December 1932.

Admittedly, the Bank of France could well afford to lose gold. In spite of this, the figures of its declining gold reserve were viewed with growing concern within and outside France. It was feared that these persistent gold withdrawals would cause panic amongst the French public and consequently a wholesale run on the banks, and a wholesale flight of capital abroad was regarded as being well within the bounds of possibility. Against this danger the French Government was utterly helpless. In order to restore confidence it would have had to balance the budget, and it was precisely the measures taken to that end which constituted the main source of danger to the stability of the franc. Fortunately for France, from the point of view of the stability of the franc, relief was forthcoming from unexpected quarters. The major crisis which began to develop in the United States in February diverted attention from her troubles. Relativity is a principle which is not confined to physical science. In matters of currency its validity has been proved over and over again. Unquestionably the budgetary situation rendered the franc vulnerable. On the other hand the banking situation in the United States rendered the dollar even more vulnerable, and relatively speaking the franc began to be regarded as a safe currency compared with the dollar. The trend of international gold movements became reversed and France succeeded in restoring some of her lost reserves. It was evident, however, that her monetary strength was merely the result of the weakness of the dollar, and that the inherent weakness of the franc was as real as ever.

Nor were any of the other gold currencies in a better position. The Swiss franc, with its note cover well in excess of 100 per cent, could not be considered to be above suspicion, and was subject to periodical attacks. The fact that the Swiss National Bank was in a position to convert the whole of the note circulation into gold and still have a substantial gold reserve left over did not in itself place the franc beyond danger. After all, the source of any possible trouble was not the danger of a wholesale conversion of bank-notes— which were legally inconvertible—but the danger of a wholesale withdrawal of foreign capital. As is well known, ever since the war Switzerland has constituted a vast haven of refuge for foreign funds. A large proportion of those who, on account of heavy taxation or the danger of a currency depreciation, desired to transfer their wealth abroad, chose Switzerland in preference to other countries. The Swiss banks have welcomed and encouraged this movement, as it has provided the country with an important source of income. During the crisis, however, the possession of large foreign balances became a doubtful blessing. Whenever the Swiss franc came under a cloud for one reason or another, such as the sudden withdrawal of German balances, or the internal troubles in November 1932, there was a danger of wholesale withdrawal of foreign funds, against which the substantial gold reserve of the National Bank would have availed very little. The adverse movement never developed sufficiently to justify fears of an immediate suspension of the gold standard, but the position was far from safe.

The Dutch guilder was in a somewhat similar position to the Swiss franc from the point of view of foreign deposits. In fact, Holland was even more vulnerable than Switzerland because of the one-sided nature of her foreign clientèle. While funds from every part of the world took refuge in the Swiss market, the predominant part of foreign balances handled by Amsterdam was of German origin. This circumstance put the guilder at the mercy of developments in Germany. Between 1931 and 1933 the guilder was subject to more attacks than any other European gold currency. On every occasion, however, the defence was successful, thanks to the resources of the Netherlands Bank and to the skilful tactics adopted by the authorities. With the assistance of the highly disciplined Dutch banks, the Dutch authorities were able to discourage bear speculation in guilders very effectively. The guilder was regarded, nevertheless, as the weakest link in the chain of gold currencies and, rightly or wrongly, it was believed that Holland would be the next country to abandon gold.

The position of Belgium was more favourable than that of either Holland or Switzerland, as there were practically no foreign balances in Brussels. On the other hand the internal position was, if anything, worse than that of either of those two countries. At one time in 1932 the belga was subject to persistent bear attacks owing to the budgetary situation. Thanks to draconian measures, however, the pressure ceased. On the other hand the movement in favour of a suspension of the gold standard was stronger in Belgium than either in France or in Holland or in Switzerland. This was because Belgian industries suffered more through the competition of depreciated sterling than any other gold country. Thanks to French assistance the Belgian authorities were able to resist adverse pressure, but it was realized by 1933 that, as there could no longer be any question of any further help from France, the belga would have to stand or fall on its own merits.

Besides these currencies, there was a number of countries which succeeded in maintaining their exchanges at par although they were not on an effective gold basis. Among others, Poland displayed a most unexpected strength throughout the crisis, and succeeded in maintaining the stability of the zloty without having to introduce any exchange restrictions. It was, therefore, a well-deserved compliment when in July 1933 the gold countries invited Poland to join their group. .

The position of the lira deserves special attention. Strictly speaking, it could not be classed with the gold currencies, as there was a very strict exchange control, in practice if not in law, in Italy, and the lira was to all intents and purposes inconvertible. Notwithstanding this, there was no difficulty in maintaining the stability of the lira. Towards the end of 1931 it was subject to a severe bear attack, but this was resisted, and afterwards the Italian authorities succeeded in making the defence of the currency water-tight. Bear speculation was made impossible by prohibiting the granting of lira credits to foreigners except for bona fide commercial purposes. For a long time the lira was stabilized at a rate slightly below par so as to increase the risk of short selling and to increase the opportunities of squeezing the bears. The export of capital was completely stopped by the exchange restrictions introduced unofficially by the Corporation of Banks. These restrictions were carried out more strictly than any official restrictions operating in other countries. Moreover, the financial relations between Italy and other countries were of such a nature as to reduce to a minimum any danger to the stability of the lira. The amount of Italy's foreign indebtedness was negligible, and the repayment of short-term debts caused no difficulty. At the same time Italy's credits abroad were also an unimportant factor, so that events in central Europe left her financially unaffected. The development of the economic situation also tended to render the lira increasingly immune from international influences. During the last few years Italy has made good progress towards economic self-sufficiency. By 1932 she was in a position to supply practically the whole of her wheat requirements from domestic sources, and the adverse balance of her visible trade was reduced to a fraction of its figure of a few years before. For this reason the decline in emigrants' remittances, which until recently had been the main support of the lira, was not seriously missed. Thanks to its isolation, the lira had become less vulnerable than almost any other currency. Although the relative strength of the Italian gold reserves bore no comparison with that of the French, Swiss, Dutch or Belgian gold reserves, the dangers of an attack on the currency were decidedly less menacing than in the case of any of those countries. Thanks to her internal economic and political organization, the likelihood of internal panics was reduced to a minimum, and the authorities were in a position to enforce emergency measures which would be doomed to failure in other countries.

In addition to the currencies on a gold basis, or stabilized in relation to gold, there is another group of currencies which, while nominally on a gold basis, are in reality depreciated. Austria, Hungary and, to a less extent, Yugoslavia, with several others, while maintaining the fiction of stability, had to allow their currencies to depreciate in the unofficial market. All these countries put up an unexpectedly good fight to maintain the depreciation within narrow limits. Thanks to the non-payment of their external debts and to exchange clearing arrangements, they were able to maintain the unofficial rate at a relatively small disparity from the official rate.

The case of Germany is of particular interest.

The maintenance of the stability of the Reichsmark has been regarded in Germany as an achievement of which a country may justly be proud. In reality it has been achieved through suspending the payment of various categories of external debt. Moreover, the stability of the Reichsmark has actually been purely fictitious. There exists in Germany a system of blocked foreign accounts which can only be used for specific purposes according to the class of the account. Reichsmarks on such accounts are dealt in abroad at a considerable discount. At one time the discount on the worst type of blocked account was nearly 50 per cent, and even at the time of writing it is about 40 per cent. In such circumstances it cannot really be said that the Reichsmark has been stable at par. Its instability and its depreciation have been skilfully disguised behind this system of blocked balances which, incidentally, enables the German Government to encourage exchange dumping whenever desirable simply by authorizing the use of blocked accounts for export purposes.

Such was the international monetary situation on the eve of the Economic Conference. With the exception of a few countries still linked to gold, currencies were depreciated everywhere, even if in some cases the depreciation was not officially acknowledged. Even those which were on a gold basis were vulnerable for one reason or another. There was no attempt of any importance being made to co-ordinate monetary policies ; and the atmosphere was charged with suspicion, hatred and mutual recrimination.

CHAPTER VIII

THE WORLD ECONOMIC CONFERENCE

THE Economic Conference of London was the first serious attempt to replace the national conception of monetary policy by an international conception. It was doomed to failure, because it was undertaken at a moment when one of the principal participants was not receptive to the ideas of monetary internationalism.

It was said in 1931 that Great Britain did not yet know that she was "broke", that Germany knew it already, and that Austria had forgotten it already. This saying, with slight modification, could be applied to the situation in 1933, when the United States did not yet know that a nationalistic monetary policy may recoil upon the nation, Great Britain was beginning to know it already, and France was beginning to forget it already. The United States, not altogether unreasonably, resented the attempt made by Great Britain and France to deprive her of the advantages of currency depreciation when both those countries had already enjoyed them. She was only just beginning to reap the pleasures of victory in the currency race. It would have been too much, indeed, to expect her to give up her winning chances. Great Britain, of course, would have liked to retain as much as possible of the advantages she had recently obtained in the depreciation race. She realized that, if the race were to continue, she would stand to lose in the next heat. As for France, she had already forgotten that it was she who started the race, and felt perfectly entitled to speak in a tone of moral indignation about any country unscrupulous enough to follow her example.

There was no reciprocal attempt on the part of the countries concerned to understand one another's position or to conciliate one another's viewpoints. It is true that each aimed at an international understanding, but this only meant that the others should accept its own point of view in full. In such circumstances it would have been little short of a miracle if the Economic Conference had led to any positive result.

During the weeks that preceded the opening of the Conference, the dollar underwent a fairly substantial depreciation, which gave rise to suspicions that the United States Government was endeavouring to improve its bargaining position and to create a *fait accompli* before the beginning of the Conference. This may or may not have been so, but the weakness of the dollar can easily be explained solely by the fact that the Washington administration had publicly declared for an inflationist policy. Having openly stated its intention of bringing about a rise in prices at all costs, and having obtained consent from Congress for powers required for inflating and devaluing the dollar, there was no need for the Government to take any deliberate steps to cause the dollar to depreciate. Market influences were in themselves quite sufficient to do the work. However it may be, the depreciation of the dollar was accompanied by outbursts of indignation in the European Press, and it was freely stated that, unless some agreement could be reached for the provisional stabilization of the exchanges during the Conference, there was no hope of any useful work being accomplished in London.

Accordingly, an attempt was made to come to an understanding for a provisional stabilization of sterling and the dollar. To that end the representatives of British, American and French central banks and Treasuries held a meeting in London, simultaneously with the opening of the Economic

Conference, to discuss the possibility of such a stabilization. On the British side, Mr. Montagu Norman and several directors of the Bank of England, as well as several high officials of the Treasury, took part in these discussions ; on the French side the Bank of France was represented by M. Farnier and M. Lacour-Gayet, and the French Treasury by M. Bizot and others ; the American delegates to this Conference, which was meant to be secret but which soon became public, included Mr. Harrison, Governor of the Federal Reserve Bank of New York, Mr. James Warburg, a member of the " brain trust ", and Professor Sprague. The latter, until a month or so previously, had occupied the post of economic adviser to the Bank of England. Soon after the suspension of the gold standard in the United States he was invited by President Roosevelt to take up a post in the United States Treasury. His appointment was received with mixed feelings by British banking circles. The optimists believed that to have someone in Washington, who regarded the British point of view with sympathy and understanding, would facilitate an understanding between Great Britain and the United States. Others, however, took a more cynical view, and expressed their apprehension that Professor Sprague, having learnt all there was to know about the technique of exchange control, would now make use of his unique experience in the service of the United States authorities against Great Britain. It was said that, on his arrival in London as one of the American negotiators, he often found it difficult to remember on which side he was negotiating. Even if he accepted his appointment with the best of intentions, he must have overestimated his influence on President Roosevelt and his notorious " brain trust ". Undoubtedly there were days, and possibly even weeks, when his influence counted for something in shaping Washington's policy, but amidst the lightning changes in that policy nobody could hope to survive as the controlling influence for any length of time.

The unofficial conference appeared to be making good progress towards the end of the first week. An understanding seemed to have been reached for a purely informal and unbinding stabilization of sterling and the dollar during the Conference. According to this so-called " gentlemen's agreement " the United States authorities were willing to keep the dollar somewhere around 4·05, reserving to themselves, however, the right to discontinue the arrangement at a moment's notice. To secure the success of the scheme it would have been necessary to keep the arrangement secret. As it transpired, however, it caused a relapse in commodity prices and a drop in Wall Street. President Roosevelt decided, therefore, to veto the arrangement so as to reassure the American public that the inflationary policy would continue. Notwithstanding his attitude, there was reason to expect that the " gentlemen's agreement " would work, in the absence of any formal undertaking on the part of the Governments, as a matter of technical day-to-day arrangement between central banks. What definitely wrecked the attempt at provisional stabilization was the attitude of France and the other gold countries in demanding a more formal and binding arrangement.

During the second half of June the gold currencies in general, and the Dutch guilder in particular, were subject to a violent bear attack. This was largely due to the assumption that, as sterling appeared to be likely to follow the depreciation of the dollar, it would become increasingly difficult for the gold countries to maintain their currencies at par. The anticipation of a suspension of the gold standard in Holland led to withdrawals of foreign deposits from Amsterdam. This coincided with a sharp controversy over the German Transfer Moratorium. There was some talk of reprisals on

the part of Holland, and this induced German holders
of guilder balances to safeguard themselves against
such a possibility by withdrawing their funds.
Under the combiñed influence of these two factors
the Nederlandsche Bank was losing gold heavily
and had to raise its Bank rate to defend the
guilder. The gold countries viewed the situation
with growing concern, and attributed the adverse
tendency to the influence of the proceedings at the
Conference. Accordingly, they decided to bring
pressure to bear upon Great Britain, and especially
upon the United States, by threatening to withdraw from the Conference unless there was a formal
undertaking that currencies would be left stable
during the Conference. While the British authorities were inclined to yield to this demand—which
was more or less in accordance with their own
intentions—the attempt aroused great indignation
in Washington. Owing to the fact that the dollar
was actually stable for a few days, and that the
existence of the " gentlemen's agreement " leaked out
—the British and American delegates at one time
mutually suspected each other of " spilling the
beans "—there was a serious setback in Wall Street
and a relapse in commodity prices.

Had the gold countries been content with the
informal arrangement between central banks, Presi-

dent Roosevelt, while disclaiming all responsibility
for it, would probably not have interfered. As it
was, he considered it necessary to come down on
it with a heavy hand. On July 4, the American
Independence Day, he despatched a note to the
American Delegation at the Economic Conference
which made it quite plain that he had not the least
intention of committing himself to any stabilization
of the dollar, however informal and temporary it
might be. The tone and contents of the note
deeply offended the delegates of the gold countries,
who decided to retaliate by wrecking the Conference. They declared that in the circumstances
negotiations on any subject within the scope of
the Conference agenda had become futile, and
demanded that the Conference should be adjourned
immediately. The next week or so was spent in
a desperate struggle to keep the Conference alive
in face of the opposition of the gold group. The
American Delegation, to avoid the impression that
it was President Roosevelt's note that had wrecked
the Conference, made a superhuman effort to keep
the Conference going. They were supported by
the British Government, which felt that, as the
host of the gathering of the representatives of 66
nations in London, the least it could do was to
prevent them from being sent home with the stigma

of failure. The delegates from the Far East and from Latin America were, in fact, indignant at the idea of having to go home, after the trouble they had taken in coming to London from such a distance, without having made any serious attempt to come to an agreement at least on minor issues.

It was widely felt that, merely because the unwillingness of the United States to stabilize the dollar prevented the Conference from becoming a 100 per cent success, there was no justification for relinquishing the chances of attaining, say, a 5 or 10 per cent success. When it came to a clash between the two parties, it was found that those in favour of continuing the Conference formed the majority. Notwithstanding this, the Governments concerned did not have the courage to declare that the Conference should go on, and that those who did not wish to participate any further were at liberty to withdraw. Had this attitude been adopted, most probably nobody would have withdrawn, for fear that they might be left out of something of importance, or that the non-gold countries, left to themselves, might form an anti-gold coalition of some sort. Rather than create ill-feeling by taking this course, it was decided to effect a compromise by adopting the principle that, though the Conference would continue to the end of July, no subject would be discussed to which objection was made by any of the participants. This decision reduced the status of the Conference to that of the Polish Parliament in centuries gone by, when one adverse vote was sufficient to veto any decision.

The only positive result of the Conference, from the point of view of the development of an international monetary policy, was the consolidation of the gold group. At first this group included France, Switzerland, Holland and Belgium only, but subsequently Italy and Poland were also admitted. Having recognized the identity of their interests in the sphere of monetary policy, these countries decided to establish closer contact with one another. Although no arrangements were made for reciprocal support, the mere moral effect of their gesture was in itself sufficient to create a favourable impression. It was one of the factors responsible for the turn in the trend of sterling in relation to gold currencies. During the first few weeks of the Conference, sterling had been inclined to appreciate against the franc, and it required some effort on the part of the authorities to prevent an appreciation and to keep sterling around 86. Early in July, however, the tide suddenly turned and, but for the intervention of the control, sterling would have depreciated considerably.

The establishment of the gold group could not in itself have brought about this fundamental change. But its effect was strengthened by the belief that sterling might follow the dollar. On one day, early in July, there was great excitement in the gossip centre of the Geological Museum. It was rumoured that Mr. Keynes had been invited to lunch with Mr. MacDonald. Knowing the type of monetary policy that Mr. Keynes had always represented, the foreign exchange market could hardly be blamed for leaping to certain conclusions on the basis of this harmless luncheon engagement. And from that time onwards sterling was subject to heavy selling pressure for at least a fortnight. The authorities, faithful to their informal promise, took it upon themselves to defend sterling against those adverse influences, and the Exchange Equalization Account sold its gold on a large scale in order to defend sterling. It is said that in the course of July it cost the British authorities something like £50,000,000 to keep sterling pegged to the franc. The Keynes-MacDonald luncheon was certainly one of the most expensive meals in history.

On July 26 the Economic Conference closed

without having achieved anything substantial. It did not bring the solution of the sterling-dollar-franc tangle any nearer. While an agreement was reached in the sub-committees on certain general principles of monetary policy, it cannot be said that on balance the Conference made any material progress towards making monetary policy to some extent subject to international understanding. From that point of view it would have been better if the example of the gold countries had been followed by the rest of the world. The grouping of countries whose monetary policies pursue more or less identical aims would have been an important step in the right direction. It is much easier to conduct negotiations between three or four groups than between a large number of individual nations. The mere fact that all countries had declared definitely their allegiance to one or other monetary policy would in itself have helped to clear the situation. The only move in that direction, however, apart from the establishment of the gold group, was the manifesto issued by the countries of the British Empire outlining a uniform monetary policy to be pursued by them.

It is said, and with good reason, that the failure of the World Conference was mainly due to the fact that monetary policy was national and not

I

international. It must be added that the Conference itself has done very little to prepare the ground for removing this obstacle to a successful attempt at an international economic understanding. Admittedly there is, on the credit side of the Conference balance sheet, the attempt to codify the rules that are to govern monetary policy. While the gulf between the leading countries remains immense so far as fundamentals are concerned, an understanding has been reached on minor points. Unquestionably this is a step in the right direction. Hitherto, it has never occurred to any country to submit the rules which it follows in its monetary policy to any international agreement. Although efforts were made in that direction in the course of the movement for co-operation between central banks, and although the working of the Bank for International Settlements was also of some assistance, the Governments of the countries concerned kept aloof from any understanding which the banking authorities may have reached. However insignificant, therefore, may be the points on which the Conference has come to an understanding, the principle has now been definitely established that questions of monetary policy can, and should, be subject to international negotiations.

On the debit side of the balance sheet there is the fact that the Conference has accentuated the existing conflict between the fundamental principles on which the monetary policies of the principal groups are based. It was because of the suspicion that he might allow himself to be persuaded into a premature stabilization that President Roosevelt had to go out of his way to accentuate his inflationist policy. It was because of the danger of being driven off the gold standard in consequence of the American attitude that the gold countries were led to emphasize, and indeed to over-emphasize, their determination to oppose any monetary experiments. It was because of the uncompromising conflict between the two policies that the British Government adopted a hesitating attitude half-way between the two. Each of the Governments was subject to much criticism for its attitude. And in the following chapters we shall try to summarize the case for and against the policies followed by America, France, and Great Britain respectively.

CHAPTER IX

THE AMERICAN CASE

IF the historian of the future bases his account of the Economic Conference of 1933 upon contemporary Press reports, it is almost inevitable that he will represent the United States as the villain of the piece. The case against the American attitude is, indeed, a very strong one. The grounds on which President Roosevelt was charged with being responsible for the failure of the Conference may be summarized as follows :

1. He deliberately went off the gold standard practically on the eve of the Conference, thereby complicating the already difficult situation.

2. He pursued a policy aiming at the depreciation of the dollar, thereby accentuating the tension and suspicion in international relations.

3. He refused to agree to a " currency truce " for the duration of the Conference, thereby making it difficult, if not impossible, for most major questions to be decided.

4. He vetoed the informal agreement arrived at by the representatives of central banks and treasuries, and allowed the dollar to be subject to most violent fluctuations during the Conference.

Unquestionably, the European statesmen who were on their way to Washington in April, and the countries which they represented, had every reason to resent the decision to go off the gold standard before the beginning of the preliminary negotiations. Even if the step was taken for purely internal reasons, it was not so desperately urgent as to make it impossible to await the result of those negotiations. As we have seen in Chapter V, there was no trace of any attack on the dollar until a few days before the actual suspension, and even then there is every reason to believe that the attack was either tolerated or encouraged, and possibly even engineered, by the American authorities themselves. It may be argued that, even if the United States had remained on the gold standard during the Conference, it would have been impossible for her to make any agreement which would preclude the possibility of a depreciation of the dollar. That depreciation was a vital necessity from an internal point of view, and nothing that the success of the Conference could have offered to the United States would have justified her Government in relinquishing the use of this remedy. Given the fact that the gold standard had to be suspended sooner or later, criticism of the United States for the choice of the moment for its suspension is hardly justified. President Roosevelt took the first opportunity, after the panicky atmosphere subsided, for making his fateful decision. Had he delayed it he might have had to suspend the gold standard immediately before, or during, the Conference.

In any case it would have been a hopeless task to try to reach an understanding about stabilization, even if the United States had remained on the gold standard. The British Government, by repeated public statements, made it quite plain, before the suspension of the gold standard in the United States, that it was not prepared to discuss the question of stabilizing sterling. In many quarters, it is true, this was regarded as sheer bluff designed to improve Great Britain's bargaining position. It was widely believed that in return for the least concession, such as a radical reduction of the war debt, or all-round tariff agreements, etc., the British Government would have been prepared to revise its point of view. This was, however, by no means the case. The settlement of war debts was but one of the preliminary conditions under which Great Britain was prepared to stabilize sterling. It was understood all along that there could be no question of stabilization until a considerable rise in world prices had taken place. Had the United States not suspended the gold standard before the Conference, and had President Roosevelt not taken up an adamant attitude on the question of stabilization, it would most probably have been Great Britain who would have gone down to posterity as the villain of the piece. As it was, the American attitude made it superfluous for Great Britain to lay any emphasis on her opposition to immediate stabilization.

The second charge against President Roosevelt's policy is that it allowed the dollar to depreciate before the Conference. As a matter of fact, the extent of the depreciation before June 12 was relatively moderate. If there is scope for criticism, it is on the ground that the depreciation was not sufficiently rapid. It may well be said that, having realized the necessity for a considerable depreciation of the dollar in order to raise internal prices, President Roosevelt ought to have acted with more determination. He had nearly two months between the suspension of the gold standard and the opening of the Economic Conference, which might have been more than enough for depreciating the exchange to the level where he wanted it ultimately to settle. Having asked for powers to devalue the dollar to the extent of 50 cents, he ought to have made use of them to their full extent before the beginning of the Conference. Admittedly, from the point of view of putting monetary policy on a basis of international co-operation, such an introductory step would have been anything but encouraging. On the other hand, if he had confronted the Conference with accomplished facts, the Conference would have had to face realities and would have had to tackle the task of coming to an understanding on the adjustment of the rest of the world to the situation created by the United States. In face of the definite fact of a 50 per cent devaluation of the dollar, it would have settled down to discuss the extent to which other countries would have to follow the American example. There would have been one fixed point, which was sadly missing throughout the Conference.

President Roosevelt and his advisers either did not know their own minds, or they were hesitating as to the way in which they could attain their end. Admittedly the situation was without precedent, and the risk of a rapid depreciation of the dollar was great. It was by no means certain that a depreciation of the dollar would be followed by a corresponding rise in internal prices. In the case · of the depreciation of sterling the effect had been totally different, and it is easy to understand why the American authorities hesitated to go too fast in a direction which might land them in a situation worse than that from which they were trying to escape. It was also reasonable to fear that, were President Roosevelt to make full immediate use of his power to devalue the dollar, the psychological factor working towards a rise in prices would cease to operate.

The most bitter attacks launched against President Roosevelt were based on his unwillingness to stabilize the dollar during the Conference. From the very outset it was made quite plain in various quarters that unless a " currency truce " was concluded for the period of the Conference, it would be impossible to discuss tariffs, exchange restrictions or any other major subjects. The gold countries were unwilling to relinquish the weapon of anti-dumping measures so long as they were not safeguarded against a further depreciation of the dollar. Nor were the financially weak countries prepared to give up their only defence, exchange restrictions, until the stability of the exchanges provided them with adequate assurances that, in doing so, they would not precipitate their collapse. This attitude was taken so much for granted that its justification was hardly contested during the Conference.

It may well be asked, however, why it would not have been possible to come to decisions about a whole range of subjects even in the absence of a currency truce. The decisions would, of course, have been made dependent on a subsequent stabilization of the dollar and sterling at a certain hypothetical level, and provisions could have been inserted for the modification of the terms of the agreements according to the actual level of the definite stabilization of both currencies. Instead of attempting this, the Conference was inclined to accept the point of view of the gold countries that nothing could be done without preliminary stabilization. If the object of this attitude was to bring pressure to bear upon the United States to stabilize without delay, it was certainly unsuccessful.

The most common argument which was used in attempting to persuade the United States to agree to the currency truce was that it would not be binding upon her future monetary policy. In the light of practical experience this argument sounds most unconvincing. It has been found that, whenever an inconvertible currency is kept stable for a while at a given level, it becomes increasingly difficult to change that level without provoking strong opposition. If the exchange remains unchanged for a few weeks or a month or two, it is generally considered to have entered the period of pre-stabilization. Any departure from that level is interpreted either as a failure of the Government's policy, or as a deliberate tampering with the exchange. Neither of these assumptions is flattering to the Government concerned. What is worse, it is exposed to pressure by all interests which favour the continuation of stability. In allowing the exchange to remain stable at a certain level for some length of time, the authorities inevitably relinquish to some extent their free hand to decide upon its future. This is exactly what President Roosevelt was not prepared to do.

It was considerations of this kind which made the commodity and security markets in the United States so strongly distrustful of any provisional stabilization. The moment the dollar remained stable for a few days (which means that its range of fluctuation was not more than five points or so) the American public began to grow anxious. It was feared that, once the dollar was kept stable for several weeks, President Roosevelt would be more inclined to consider the idea of stabilization favourably. As the rise in commodity prices was due, not to any genuine consumer demand, but to the anticipation of a further depreciation of the dollar, the likelihood of a stabilization was bound to provoke a strong reaction. This is exactly what happened over and over again : and the President, anxious to maintain the upward trend, arrived at the conclusion that it was of importance to avoid making it appear in any way as if he intended to stabilize. It was for this reason that he decided to veto even the informal arrangement which was concluded by the American Delegation in London.

It would, indeed, have been too much to expect the United States to stabilize the dollar at about 20 or 25 per cent under its parity. The depreciation was not nearly sufficient to bring about the rise in prices which was essential to place the United States on a stable financial basis. It is true that the rapid rise in wheat prices brought considerable relief to the farmers, so that part of the rural mortgages which became frozen through the slump were becoming liquid again. Had there been any reasonable hope of maintaining wheat prices at the peak reached in July, it might

have become superfluous, from the point of view
of the farm mortgages, to depreciate the dollar
any further, especially as farmers were also to
receive direct subsidies. There was, however, no
justification for assuming that, on the basis of the
then prevailing depreciation of the dollar, the
general price level would rise sufficiently to make
it possible for wheat prices to remain at such a
height. Nor were rural mortgages the only source
of difficulty. Urban mortgages constitute a much
larger item in the nation's indebtedness than rural
mortgages, and their unfreezing is a much more
difficult process. While a rise in wheat, the most
elastic of commodities, is sufficient to provide
considerable relief to farmers, it requires a lasting
and substantial rise in the general price level to
bring about a corresponding movement in the
value of town property. In order to enable the
railroad companies to bear their burden of indebtedness, a considerable rise in prices would be necessary. It is also advisable to bear in mind that
stabilization, no matter at what level and at what
time, is bound to be accompanied by a relapse
in commodity prices. Thus, if the total increase
aimed at is, say, 60 per cent, it is necessary to
allow a safety margin of, say, another 20 per cent,
so as to make sure that after the reaction that

follows stabilization there will still be a net rise of 60 per cent on balance.

Evidently the extent of the rise in prices in July 1933 was not nearly large enough from this point of view. Owing to the discrepancy between the rise in the price of produce and of manufactures, the index numbers varied widely in their estimates of the rise, but the average was certainly not more than 15 per cent higher than in April.

Would President Roosevelt have been justified in jeopardizing a further rise for the sake of the success of the Conference? In the first place, even if he had yielded completely, there would still have been immense controversial issues left over and the success of the Conference would still have been doubtful. But, even if the willingness of the United States to stabilize had led to a complete agreement on all points, the result, from an American point of view, would not have justified the sacrifice of the advantages obtained through a further rise in prices. The opposition with which the British Government's proposals for raising prices, spineless and innocuous as they were, were met, duly indicated how much, or how little, could be expected in that direction of a successful conclusion of the Conference. The gold group was dead against any monetary measures by which a rise in prices could be encouraged. The British Government, favouring the idea of a rise, was opposed to any practical measure which could possibly have contributed to bring it about. One of the characters in Oscar Wilde's *Dorian Gray* once remarked that he would do anything to maintain his youth except getting up early, leading a moderate life, or taking exercise. This was approximately the attitude of the British Government towards bringing about a rise of prices. It was opposed to unbalancing the budget, financing public works, or a deliberate depreciation of the currency. What it was prepared to do was to keep money cheap and exhort the bankers from time to time to lend money to a public which was unwilling to borrow. The experience of the twelve months that preceded the Conference ought to have taught them that cheap money in itself does not cause prices to rise. And to think that even these tame and highly inadequate suggestions were received with scorn and indignation by the gold countries ! It is no wonder that the United States Government abandoned all hope of obtaining a rise in prices through the success of the Conference. It was fully realized in Washington that the only basis on which an agreement in London was conceivable was on the strict rules of orthodoxy.

An agreement in London would have meant deflation or, at the most, stabilization on the existing level. As, however, half the United States was hopelessly and irredeemably bankrupt on the basis of that level, it was vital for her to raise prices before stabilizing. Any revival of international trade that might have followed the removal of exchange control and trade barriers would have been far from sufficient to save the United States if half her population had not been made solvent by an adequate rise in prices. In the circumstances, no blame could be attached to President Roosevelt even if it was his attitude towards stabilization that wrecked the Conference.

CHAPTER X

THE FRENCH CASE

In the previous chapter we arrived at the conclusion that the American attitude was the right one. As the French attitude, shared by the other gold countries, was diametrically opposed to the American attitude, it appears on the surface that the approval of one must necessarily mean the disapproval of the other. And yet, at the risk of being accused of inconsistency, we are prepared to maintain that both attitudes were right. If we qualify this statement by saying that the American attitude was absolutely right from an American point of view, and the French attitude was absolutely right from a French point of view, then the contradiction disappears. It is easy to pronounce judgment in a case in which one of the parties is obviously in the right, and the other obviously in the wrong. It is much more difficult to take sides when both parties are equally right, only from a different point of view. Such a conflict of two just causes contains the elements of classical tragedy.

In previous chapters we pointed out that to relieve the burden of debtors by means of a rise in prices was of vital importance for the United States. The same considerations did not exist for France. The devaluation of the franc to one-fifth of its pre-war value had already brought all the relief that was needed in order to make public and private indebtedness bearable. Deliberately to repeat the same experience once more could not possibly be justified by any urgent considerations. France could carry on quite well on the basis of the existing price level, and her population would thus benefit to the full extent from any revival of business activity that might be attained through the removal of trade barriers. While the French budgetary situation was anything but enviable, a trade revival could easily put it right without the necessity for cutting down the burden of public debt by inflation.

Admittedly, French trade would benefit to no slight extent by the stimulus of rising prices. The French farmers would become prosperous, without having to be subsidized by the Government, through a sustained rise in world prices. The prosperity, apparent or real, that always accompanies rising prices would benefit French luxury industries at least as much as any other interests. Last but not least, the Government and Parliament would find it incomparably easier to tackle the problems of budgetary equilibrium, Treasury liquidity, and debt conversion.

Even after admitting all this, the weight of argument is, from a purely French point of view, overwhelmingly against a policy of inflation. The French public had already one inflationary experience during 1923-6, and it can hardly be blamed for not wanting another. In France the rentier is both politically and financially the backbone of the nation. It is the proverbial thrift of this class to which the inherent wealth and prosperity of the French people are mainly due. It is owing to the fundamental conservatism of this class that France is more immune than almost any other country from violent political changes. After the war, the interests of this class were sacrificed for the sake of reconstruction and to secure an expansion of production. By undertaking the reconstruction of devastated areas without awaiting the receipt of reparations from Germany, the French Governments that followed each other during that period were responsible for inflation on an immense scale. It was unthinkable that this inflation could have been liquidated through any other means than devaluation. A return to pre-war parity was out of the question, and it was only the degree of the devaluation which had to be decided upon between 1926 and 1928. The decision of 1928 ruthlessly sacrificed the interests of the rentier class. The experience of a pre-stabilization period of eighteen months conclusively proved that France could well have afforded to stabilize the franc at a higher level. A stabilization around, say, 100 francs to the pound could have safely been undertaken from an international point of view. For the sake of political and commercial advantages the French Government decided, however, to choose a lower level. The patriotism of the rentier was put to a very severe test, but eventually he allowed himself to be persuaded that his sacrifice was a necessity. In the meantime the fall in prices has more or less made good what the rentier lost in purchasing power through the unjustified undervaluation of the franc. In spite of this, no French Government would care to repeat the experience.

It is not only the rentiers who are opposed to a policy of inflation. The mentality of the whole French nation is such as to make it impossible for any Government or Parliament deliberately to bring about a rise in prices. The French public is mortified at the idea of *la vie chère*. It is prepared to put up with higher prices if it is necessary for the sake of its peasant classes, but no Government would ever persuade the French public to suffer voluntarily an inflationary policy for the sake of such a vague aim as an international trade revival. Any Government which wants to remain in office—and what Government does not?—must take account of the inherent deflationistic mentality of the French nation.

It is not merely the injustice and inevitable unpopularity of another devaluation of the franc that deters the French Government from abandoning the path of orthodoxy. The financial and commercial prestige of France is at stake also. One of the reasons why the post-war inflation and the devaluation of the franc were so easily forgotten was because it was generally assumed that the circumstances in which they occurred would never recur again. The expense of the war and of the reconstruction of north-eastern France were extremely special circumstances which constituted a fair defence against any imputation of unsound post-war finance in France. The public, both in France and abroad, was convinced that with the stabilization of 1928 France had turned over a new leaf, and that she would never relapse into the vice of inflation. Should the French Government, contrary to this assumption, yield to the lure of inflation, the result of this disappointment would be a strong and deep-set distrust. This time it would not be so easy to heal the wound as it was in 1928. While the United States and Great Britain may be able to devalue their currencies, France and other countries which have already devalued theirs could ill afford to do so a second time. The loss of financial prestige would be felt particularly keenly by France because it would inevitably be accompanied by a decline in her political prestige. The strength of her financial position since 1928 has done at least as much to establish her prestige on the Continent as the strength of her army. It would only be with the greatest reluctance that any French Government would care to relinquish such an asset.

Among the countries which grouped themselves round France in the matter of monetary policy, Holland and Switzerland occupy a special position. Apart from a relatively brief and moderate lapse during and after the war, their currencies have never departed from gold. They regained their pre-war parities amidst the turmoils of post-war inflation and retained them in spite of the present world crisis. Both of them, however, have had to pay a heavy price for it. Holland and her colonies have had to suffer the disadvantages common to

all raw-material and food-producing countries and
the handicap of unfavourable exchanges in addition.
Switzerland has lost a large part of her tourist traffic
owing to the prohibitive exchange rate of the Swiss
franc. Both countries hope, however, to be com-
pensated for these passing inconveniences by the
long-period moral effect of the stability of their
currencies. Both Amsterdam and the Swiss market
have in the past entertained the ambition to attract
a large volume of international banking business.
They have, in fact, been selected as the refuge
for large amounts of Central European and other
foreign capital. Should the guilder and the Swiss
franc retain their stability when sterling and the
dollar lost theirs, both countries would have a good
chance of retaining and strengthening their position
as international financial centres. In the long run
the benefits obtained from this function would
amply compensate them for their immediate losses.
This is probably the main reason why the Swiss
and Dutch Governments have so far resisted the
strong pressure brought to bear upon them by local
economic interests to relieve their difficulties by suspending the gold standard.

The position of Belgium shows more similarity
to that of France than to that of Holland or Switzerland. Having devalued her currency to an even

greater extent than France, the Belgian Government does not wish to repeat the expedient if there is any way of avoiding it. Although the Belgian heavy industries suffer a good deal through the depreciation of sterling, the Government is not prepared to sacrifice the stability of the belga for their sake.

The position of Italy is totally different from that of the other gold countries. Signor Mussolini has succeeded in reorganizing the nation both politically and economically by means of arousing a spirit of patriotic enthusiasm in the nation. The amazing progress which Italy has made is built largely, if not exclusively, upon Signor Mussolini's immense personal prestige. It is feared that, should he allow the lira to collapse, it would be highly detrimental to his prestige and would therefore affect most unfavourably the prospects of maintaining and expanding the progress so far attained. Moreover, the Government is anxious to avoid anything that would discourage the development of the saving instinct among the population, which has made a remarkable advance during the last few years. Scarcity of capital has always been a severe handicap to Italy's ambitions to develop into a first-rate power. The creation of a large and wealthy rentier class similar to that existing in France is considered, therefore, to be of great importance for Italy. The success of several recent Government-guaranteed issues, which were taken up eagerly by the public, shows that satisfactory progress is being made in that direction. But depreciation of the lira would inevitably check the progress and would discourage the tendency to a great extent. That is why Signor Mussolini is so adamant in insisting on the maintenance of the lira at its present parity.

The sixth member of the gold group is Poland ; and her case for maintaining stability is strengthened by the fact that she has had to devalue her currency already on two previous occasions since the restoration of her independence. The first attempt at stabilization having failed, Poland had to devalue the zloty in 1924. Right from the beginning of the crisis Poland put up a gallant fight to prevent the recurrence of that experience, and her admission to the exclusive group of gold countries was a well-deserved recognition of those efforts.

The policy of the gold group was supported at the Economic Conference by a number of outsiders as well as its own members. Some of them, like the countries of the Little Entente, considered it their duty, as the political satellites of France, to support whatever policy she chose to advocate. In other cases a fair degree of opportunism was clearly evident. Nevertheless, it is impossible to deny that those who were in favour of stability at all costs had a strong case. They were just as right from their own point of view as the United States was right from hers.

CHAPTER XI

THE BRITISH CASE

HAVING thus stated the case for currency depreciation as represented by the United States, and the
case for stability as represented by France and the
gold group, we must now try to analyse the British
attitude. It is a much more difficult task than to
analyse the case for and against depreciation because ; while the policy of both the extreme groups
was clear, that of Great Britain was most indistinct.
Ever since the dollar began to depreciate on a
large scale, Great Britain was confronted with an
awkward dilemma. As a nation dependent on her
exports she was drawn towards a policy aiming at
the depreciation of sterling in sympathy with the
dollar. As an inherently orthodox nation, with a
high standard of commercial morality, the idea of
any deliberate action to depreciate her currency
was repugnant to her. The choice between following the dollar or linking up sterling with the gold
currencies was therefore by no means easy. There

was an impressive array of argument both for and against following the dollar, and the position of those with whom the decision rested was far from enviable.

The following is a list of the principal arguments used by those advocating that sterling should follow the dollar :

1. The appreciation of sterling in terms of the dollar would deal a severe blow to Great Britain's trade balance.

2. A depreciation of sterling would reduce the real burden of public debt in the way which is the least painful to creditors.

3. A depreciation of sterling would provide a most welcome relief to debtors both at home and abroad.

4. In order to be able to stabilize sterling without the risk of another collapse, it would be desirable to bring it down to a lower level.

The following are the principal arguments in favour of linking sterling to the gold countries :

1. London's prestige as an international financial centre would suffer through a prolonged instability of sterling.

2. The invisible exports represented by the yield of British investments abroad would decline considerably through a devaluation of sterling.

3. A prolonged instability of sterling would postpone economic recovery, which can only be attained through a return of confidence.

4. A further depreciation of sterling might result in a collapse of hitherto stable currencies, and this might deprive Great Britain of the commercial advantages she has hitherto enjoyed through the depreciation of sterling.

Let us try to examine these arguments. The importance of avoiding an overvaluation of sterling in terms of the dollar cannot be overestimated. The United States is our most important commercial rival in international trade, and a sterling-dollar rate which places our exporting industries at a disadvantage against their American competitors would result in a strongly adverse change in our trade balance. A great deal has been said about the difficulties of ascertaining the economic parities of sterling. Without aiming at calculating it to the cent, it is beyond doubt that at 3.50 sterling was decidedly undervalued. It is equally beyond doubt that at 4.50 sterling is grossly overvalued. It is true that by the time sterling rose from 3.50 to 4.50 the economic parity had also changed through a rise in prices in the United States. We must bear in mind, however, that this rise was due almost exclusively to the advance in prices of primary produce, while prices of manufactures, with which our exporters are concerned, moved only very slightly. The fears of serious repercussions on British export trade in case of a further deprecia-tion of the dollar were therefore by no means exaggerated. This argument carried considerable weight in the controversy, especially as it was pointed out that any deterioration of the trade balance would in any case result in a depreciation of sterling. It is better to arrive at that result through deliberate policy rather than be compelled to arrive at it by the force of circumstances.

The second argument in favour of depreciation —that it would relieve the burden of public debt —was less popular than the first. To depreciate the currency in order to reduce the real value of public debt is nothing but a disguised default, and as such it is rejected with scorn by ninety-nine Englishmen out of a hundred. And yet, after they recovered from their first indignation, they could not help recognizing its convincing force. It is beyond a doubt that, on the basis of the present price level, a public debt of nearly seven milliard pounds (after allowing for a reduction of our war debt to the United States) would constitute an unbearable burden for the next 100 years or more. So long as this burden is not mitigated in some way

or other it will be a Damocles' Sword over the head
of the British nation and might even sooner or later
endanger the stability of the international economic
system. It is tempting to argue on the lines that,
now that we are off the gold standard, it would
be a mistake to miss this unique opportunity for
solving the problem of excessive public debt once
and for all. As the currency is in any case in the
melting-pot, and we are at liberty to choose the
rate at which it will be stabilized, we may as well
choose a rate at which the public debt would no
longer constitute an unbearable burden. It is unthinkable that, on the basis of this argument alone,
any British Government would ever decide in favour
of a depreciation of sterling. It is, however, one
thing to seek relief by deliberate depreciation, and
another thing to obtain it under the force of circumstances as a result of the depreciation policy adopted
by another country. As by the force of circumstances sterling will have to follow the depreciation
of the dollar in any case, the inflationary policy
of the United States will be responsible indirectly for
the depreciation of sterling ; we are thus in a lucky
position, as someone else is doing our " dirty work ".

The argument that a depreciation of sterling
would provide a relief to debtors other than the
British Government carries but little weight in the

case of internal debts. While in the United States the excessive burden of internal indebtedness was the chief cause of, and justification for, the policy aiming at the depreciation of the dollar, in Great Britain internal private indebtedness is, generally speaking, not excessive. There are undoubtedly exceptions, such as, for instance, the railway companies, to which a relief in the form of currency depreciation would come as a godsend. The relative importance of these cases is, however, far from sufficient to influence the monetary policy of the country. On the other hand, it is beginning to be realized that the increase in the burden of foreign debts owing to Great Britain through the fall of prices is in the long run detrimental to the interests of the creditors themselves, and that from that point of view a depreciation of the currency may provide an ideal solution. So long as the debtors kept on paying and the creditors continued to receive their dividends in a currency with increased purchasing power, all was well. When, however, the increase in the real burden of indebtedness compelled a large number of debtors to default, the creditors began to realize that they stood to lose by this arrangement. In most cases it is certain that, so long as the present price level subsists, the debtors will never resume payment in full.

The choice lies between agreeing to a reduction of principal and interest of the debt and enabling the debtor to pay in full through raising the price level by monetary means. In either case the creditors will have to consent to sacrifices, but the latter solution is decidedly less painful than the former. It is preferable to receive the same amount of pounds with a diminished purchasing power, than to receive a reduced amount of pounds. The advantage of the easier solution is not merely psychological, although the significance of the fact that the patients barely notice when they are being operated upon should not be underrated. In a very large number of individual cases there is, in addition, a direct material advantage in choosing currency depreciation in preference to a cut in the sterling amount receivable. Many holders of foreign bonds have contracted loans in terms of sterling on the security of those bonds. If sterling depreciates, the real value of their bonds declines, but so does the real burden of their liability. If the sterling amount of the loans is reduced by agreement with the debtors, then the value of the bonds declines while that of the loans contracted against them remains unchanged. The conclusion is that from the point of view of holders of foreign bonds currency depreciation is decidedly a more favourable solution

L

than partial default or debt reduction by arrangement.

Lastly, those in favour of a further depreciation of sterling maintain that the lower the level at which it is stabilized the safer it is from the risk of a second collapse. There is a great deal of truth in this conception, although if carried to extremes it may lead to a currency war or a depreciation race which, in the long run, will defeat the object of the policy.

The City is the main stronghold of the opposition to the idea of allowing sterling to depreciate further and to fluctuate. This is only natural, for, from the bankers' point of view, it is of vital importance that the currency of an international banking centre should be stable. In order to recover her old position as the world's banker, Great Britain will have to stabilize her currency. After several years of inactivity, the banking community is naturally impatient to see sterling stabilized at the earliest possible moment. It is argued by bankers and their spokesmen that, unless sterling is stabilized at an early date, London will lose for ever her chances of recovering her old leading position. This argument is decidedly a gross overstatement of an otherwise good case. The experience of the last few years has conclusively proved that, when London is unable to fulfil her function as the world's banker, no other centre is able, or willing, to take her place. It is evident that neither New York nor Paris nor the minor continental centres are equipped with the same technical facilities which secured the lead for London in the past. If London is prevented by adverse circumstances from fulfilling her function as the world's banker, it means simply that the rôle remains unfilled. The moment adverse circumstances cease to operate, and London is in a position to resume her old position, she can do so unhampered by her rivals. Whenever sterling is stabilized, whether it is to-morrow or in three years' time, London can become once more the world's banker. In fact, her position will be much more secure if the stabilization of sterling is not premature and the ground is well prepared for that step. If sterling is stabilized at the wrong time and at the wrong level, the experience of 1925–31 may repeat itself. London would be handicapped in fulfilling the rôle of the world's international banking centre by the vulnerability of sterling. Thus, from the point of view of restoring London as the world's banking centre the weight of argument is against, rather than for, stabilizing sterling prematurely in relation to the gold currencies.

But, even if it were desirable from the point of

view of London's international financial position
to stabilize sterling immediately, the question may
arise whether this is to the interest of the whole
country or that of the City only. If the desire of
the banking community to resume its function in
the field of international finance were to come into
conflict with the interests of production and trade,
then there can be no hesitation as to which side
would win. Without underrating the relative importance of London's international banking functions, it ought to be borne in mind that the income
derived from it is only a fraction of the nation's
total income. In a normal year London's profit
on international banking activity does not exceed
£10,000,000, and is most probably rather below
that figure if we allow for losses during bad years.
Even if immediate stabilization were in accordance
with the interests of the banking community, but
were against the interests of trade, the balance of
argument would be decidedly against immediate
stabilization.

We have seen above that one of the arguments
in favour of a policy of following the dollar is that
it would give the necessary relief to our foreign
debtors to enable them to pay the full sterling
amounts of their debts. This same argument is
used also by those who oppose a further deprecia-

tion of sterling. They point out that as a creditor nation it would be against our interests to allow sterling to depreciate, for, in doing so, we should reduce the income which we derive from foreign investment. We have already said above that in this respect the choice lies, not between being paid in full or not being paid in full, but between an open reduction of the debt and a disguised, less painful, form of its reduction. If the creditors were in a position to make the debtors pay in full by simply refusing to consent to any reduction, the argument of the opponents of depreciation would carry some weight. As it is, however, it is plain that the income obtained from overseas investments is bound to decline whether sterling is allowed to depreciate or not.

One of the most popular arguments in favour of an immediate stabilization is that it would terminate the crisis by restoring confidence. It is maintained that the policy of postponing stabilization until after a rise in commodity prices is mistaken, for a lasting rise in prices can only take place through a return of confidence, and confidence can only return as a result of a restoration of monetary stability. On the surface this line of reasoning sounds convincing. In reality, however, those who pursue it are guilty of the elementary fallacy of begging the question. They take it for granted that the stabilization of currencies would restore confidence sufficiently to bring about a trade revival and a rise of prices. This is exactly the question which is open to grave doubt. Would the world trust a stability based on a price level which makes it impossible for most debtors to discharge their liabilities in full ? Would it not be wiser to postpone stabilization until it can be achieved at a level on the basis of which most debtors resume their solvency ? This is purely a matter of opinion ; there is no way of testing the feelings of the public on the subject. In our view it is more in accordance with common sense to be on the safe side and postpone stabilization until prices have risen to a reasonable level. It is true that to raise prices by non-monetary means to the desired level is bordering on the impossible. That is why we should not shrink from discarding our orthodoxy and raising prices by monetary means.

Admittedly a prolonged instability of sterling carries the risk of further complications in the sphere of international finance. It might result in a collapse of hitherto stable currencies. This argument is freely used by the opponents of a further depreciation of sterling, on the ground that it would be detrimental to world recovery as well as to the immediate commercial interests of Great Britain. From an international point of view the suspension of the gold standard by France and other countries would undoubtedly present a number of serious inconveniences. It would, however, have the compensating advantage of carrying further the liquidation of excessive indebtedness from which the world is suffering. Moreover, taking a long view, it would not be a sound state of affairs if the franc and several other currencies were to remain relatively overvalued. The restoration of the gold standard on such an uneven basis would result in a persistent outflow of gold from the countries with overvalued currencies, and sooner or later the history of 1931 would repeat itself. From the point of view of the immediate interests of British export trade the depreciation of the currencies of our competitors would unquestionably deal a heavy blow to us. The depreciation of the Reichsmark would particularly affect our export trade. From this point of view, however, it ought to be remembered that, as a result of the discount on blocked marks which can be used for export purposes, German exporters already enjoy that advantage to a great extent, so that an official depreciation of the Reichsmark would only confirm the existing state of affairs. In any case, if the position of overvalued currencies proves to be untenable, in the long run, the British export trade will have to pay the penalty sooner or later for any advantage it has enjoyed through an excessive undervaluation of sterling in relation to those currencies.

The balance of argument is decidedly against an immediate stabilization, which explains the British Government's attitude in refusing to commit itself in that direction. At the same time the arguments against following the dollar were sufficiently weighty to make responsible quarters hesitate before embarking upon that policy. Hence the compromise of keeping sterling pegged to the franc so long as this was possible, without undertaking any commitments to that effect. In finance, as in politics, situations arise in which logic has to be discarded in the face of practical necessity.

CHAPTER XII

CONCLUSION

WE are now confronted with the most difficult part of our task. It was comparatively easy to state the case for and against national and international monetary policies. It was not difficult to justify the American, French and British case from the respective points of view of the countries concerned. It is tempting to leave it at that and, taking the line of least resistance, to conclude that there can be no compromise between such conflicting viewpoints. We do not share the pessimism of those who believe that civilization is bound to collapse unless some solution is found. We are convinced that a disentanglement is only a question of time, and that it will take place in spite of the inability of statesmen to come to an understanding.

In order to be able to conclude the book in a positive tone by suggesting what ought to be done instead of trusting fate and the endurance of mankind to put up with a great deal more before muddling through, it would be helpful first to visualize what is likely to happen if no deliberate solution is found. The situation is extremely complicated and entirely without precedent. In such circumstances making forecasts is a risky and thankless task. Events are developing with such dramatic rapidity, and kaleidoscopic changes in the situation are following each other in such close succession, that anybody who dares to prophesy runs the risk of being contradicted by events by the time his forecasts are published.

There are, fortunately, several basic facts in the situation which can to a great extent be relied upon. Although in the evolution of such an unprecedented crisis it is very often the unexpected that happens, there is still a certain consistency in the course of events.

It is, for instance, as certain as anything can be in the sphere of economics, that nothing short of a miracle can prevent an inflationary rise of prices in the United States in the near future. This statement would have been regarded as a truism two months ago, when it was the declared policy of the United States administration to raise prices by every possible means at its disposal. In the meantime, however, the situation has become more complicated. The comparatively simple policy of inflationism formerly pursued has been replaced by the so-called National Recovery scheme, which concentrates its efforts upon raising wages to a level corresponding to the rise in prices so far achieved rather than upon any further rise in prices.

If there were reasonable hopes that this policy could succeed, the likelihood of a further depreciation of the dollar would be highly doubtful. As it is, however, it is exceedingly improbable that President Roosevelt can attain his end without a further dose of currency depreciation. In compelling industrial enterprise to pay higher wages out of non-existent profits in anticipation of future trade recovery, he is putting the cart before the horse. It is by no means certain that the additional purchasing power created by higher wages will adequately compensate industries for the sacrifices to which they have had to consent. Should the idea prove to be a failure it might endanger the very existence of a large number of leading industrial enterprises. The only way to save them from ruin would then be through inflationary measures which, by raising prices, would enable them once again to work profitably in spite of the higher wages and shorter hours.

It seems, therefore, that all the Recovery Scheme has done is unnecessarily to complicate the situation and to cause further delay in the inevitable process of inflation. Even if the Government were to decide to avoid inflation at all costs it would be powerless against the trend of developments. Inflation in the United States is bound to come whether with or without the consent of the Administration. This is one of the basic facts on which we may safely rely in trying to form an opinion on future prospects.

Given the view that the dollar is likely to depreciate further, it is a foregone conclusion that sterling cannot remain for any length of time in the vicinity of its present level. It is true that six months ago even a rate of 3·75 would have been considered as too high, while any suggestion of a rate of $4·00 would have been rejected without a moment's hesitation : and that none the less at the present time even the actual level of 4·50 is considered workable in some quarters, provided that internal prices in the United States continue to rise and that the gold currencies remain at par. There must be, however, a limit beyond which the situation would become obviously untenable. Nobody could seriously suggest that a rate of $6·00 or $7·00 to the pound could ever be agreed upon. Should sterling ever be stabilized on such a basis the result would be an irresistible drain of

gold from London and other European centres to
the United States, and before many years we should
once more be driven off the gold standard.

Assuming, as we do, that the dollar will depreciate
further, it is only consistent to assume also that
sterling will follow the dollar to some extent. To
take this course will be inevitable from the point
of view of Imperial unity also. Canada could
never agree to break away altogether from the
dollar, and to force her to break away from sterling
would be a grave mistake from an Imperial point
of view. Even if our authorities were to try to
keep away from the dollar, beyond a certain point
the deterioration of our trade balance would in
any case automatically cause a depreciation of
sterling.

We can thus safely assume that both the dollar
and sterling will depreciate in the near future.
The question is whether in such circumstances
France and the other gold countries will be able
to retain their exchanges at par. Undoubtedly the
technical position of the French franc is strong.
Notwithstanding the huge budget deficit there is
no imminent danger of a collapse of the franc.
Nor is it by any means certain that in consequence
of the depreciation of sterling and dollar the French
trade balance would deteriorate to such an extent

as to cause the suspension of the gold standard. It should be remembered that France depends upon her foreign trade to a much less extent than Great Britain. If, in consequence of exchange dumping, her trade balance threatens to become strongly adverse, she can correct it by the application of quotas, exchange clearing arrangements and barter transactions.

The weakness of the franc lies in the possibility of unfavourable psychological developments. In addition to the bad impression caused by the budget deficit, pessimism may be aroused through the suspension of the gold standard by some other member of the gold bloc. Holland, Switzerland and Belgium stand to lose much more through exchange dumping than France, for none of them is nearly so self-sufficient economically. If any of these countries is compelled by an adverse trade balance to abandon gold, it would inevitably lead to a flight from the franc. The French public is extremely sensitive to an outflow of gold, and it is to be feared that, should the flight from the franc result in a heavy outflow, it might create a panic which would end in the suspension of the gold standard. For the moment there is no danger; in fact, during the period while sterling and dollar are depreciating, the franc is likely to gain in strength by contrast with those currencies. Its dangers will begin when both sterling and dollar have reached the point which may reasonably be regarded as their lowest level. Their undervaluation, and the assumption that a further depreciation is most unlikely, will then result in a flight to the pound and to the dollar. In the face of such a movement the resistance of the gold currencies, already weakened by adverse trade balances, might well be broken.

It seems, therefore, extremely probable that unless an international agreement is arrived at during the next few months, the gold countries will be driven off the gold standard eventually notwithstanding their determination to remain on gold. Once they suspend the gold standard their currencies are likely to slump heavily. It is true that technically a relatively moderate fall would be sufficient to restore equilibrium. To judge by our experience of the dollar's movements, however, it seems probable that, for psychological reasons, all currencies will seek adjustment to the sterling-dollar level. Much against their wish the gold countries will then have to put up with the dreaded rise in prices.

As far as it is humanly possible to foresee future developments amidst the present uncertainty, this forecast stands a good chance of being confirmed by events. The realization of this facilitates the task of indicating the line of action which ought to be adopted. If the gold countries had a good chance of being able to maintain the stability of their currencies, and of compelling both the United States and Great Britain to stabilize, their policy would unquestionably be regarded as the right one. As it is, however, they are evidently fighting a losing battle. The tendencies working towards a general depreciation of currencies are much stronger than those working towards stabilization. In a way this is a natural development. If no solution is found for the economic deadlock, it will solve itself automatically through the inevitable depreciation of currencies. Anti-inflationist propaganda, in its efforts to avert the inevitable, is at pains to represent inflation as being equivalent to the destruction of civilization. Those who have an elementary knowledge of the obvious facts of post-war financial history must realize, however, how absurd this contention is. Even in countries where inflation had reached the extreme stage, as in Germany for example, civilization survived. As there can be no question of a recurrence of extreme inflation in any country—circumstances are now totally different—any suggestion that inflation might result in revolution, anarchy, the destruction of the bases of material welfare and of moral progress, is sheer nonsense. As inflation, generally speaking, favours the productive classes, it is likely to prevent rather than cause revolution and anarchy. The lightning-conductor of inflation may even prove the saviour of modern Western civilization, for the forces working towards inflation would make sufficient progress to save the situation in time if it threatened to collapse under the weight of the economic crisis. Admittedly the reprieve provided by inflation is both artificial and temporary. But even if we admit that the recovery is bound to be followed by a worse crisis, it is to be welcomed, for, after all, it is better to " go to the dogs " in 1938 than in 1934. But, even if every one of us were determined anti-inflationists, and would prefer to be ruined by deflation rather than be saved by inflation, all the same we should be saved through inflation even against our will.

The choice lies not between inflating or not inflating but between regulating the inevitable process of inflation or allowing it to run loose after it has broken down our resistance. In the first case we should keep inflation under control, thereby minimizing its adverse effects. In the second case inflation would be at liberty to do its very worst.

This is the reason why an international agreement for a co-ordinated depreciation of all currencies is of vital importance. In coming to an agreement as to the extent to which various currencies should be depreciated or devalued, many of the evil consequences of depreciation could be forestalled. From the point of view of prestige, it would be much less derogatory for the gold countries to devalue their currencies as part of an international agreement, than to be forced off the gold standard one after the other. They would be able to spare their populations the shock and the evil effects of currency fluctuations ; by devaluing deliberately instead of allowing their currencies to find their own levels, the chaotic conditions of a depreciation race could be avoided. Lastly, there is a reasonable chance that the levels of the various exchanges, if chosen under the terms of a general stabilization agreement, would not be in glaring disequilibrium with each other. Admittedly, it is extremely difficult to ascertain the economic value of any currency, but the fact that all the interests concerned would be represented at the discussions would at any rate reduce the likelihood of one country, or one group of countries, being victimized by other countries choosing an unjustifiable level for their currencies.

We have reached a stage when nationalism in

the sphere of monetary policy threatens to lead to chaos and destruction. Whatever passing advantages a nation may secure by managing its monetary policy on a basis of purely national considerations, they could not be advantages such as would compensate it for the disastrous consequences of the uncontrolled inflation which is the alternative to international monetary agreement. The time has arrived when monetary nationalism is bound to recoil on the nation that practises it, and defeat its own object. If the nations wish to secure the success of the second part of the Economic Conference, they will have to come to London in a very different spirit from the one prevailing in June 1933. An agreement on the principles of international stabilization will have to be reached on the basis of " give and take " in a spirit of mutual understanding. Once it is realized that, for internal considerations of vital importance, the United States is obliged to depreciate the dollar further, the task of the other nations is to adjust their currencies to the new level of the dollar. There is no room for hard bargaining in that respect. Any nation which tries to secure itself undue advantages ought to realize that such a policy is bound to bring its own revenge in the long run.

There are unquestionably difficulties of a technical nature which would have to be overcome even if the main principle were agreed upon. For example, the mere idea of a discussion of co-ordinated devaluation of currencies would place the gold countries in a most awkward position. There would be a flight from the gold currencies which might compel them to suspend the gold standard and allow their exchanges to fluctuate during the negotiations. In order to avoid this, it would be necessary for the gold countries to decide upon devaluation to a provisional level before the beginning of the second Conference. Provided that the level chosen were low enough there would be no difficulty in maintaining the stability of the currencies during the Conference.

It is often argued that the devaluation of the dollar would not necessarily lead to higher prices. All that a change of the mint parity would do would be to increase the gold basis for the potential credit expansion. Unless there were an actual demand for additional credit, the result would be merely the flooding of money markets with short-term funds. It ought to be borne in mind, however, that the restoration of international monetary stability at a level at which most currencies are entirely above suspicion would go a long way towards restoring confidence. This, again, would lead to an increase in business activity, and before long there would be no lack of genuine demand for the additional resources made available through the revaluation of the gold reserve. Prices would inevitably rise until they found their new equilibrium, the level of which depends on the rate of stabilization and upon the monetary policy pursued by the leading countries after devaluation.

It may be argued that such a rise in prices will inevitably be followed by a fall, just as the rise during and after the war was followed by a relapse. A change in the monetary unit through devaluation would, however, prevent prices from ever declining to their present level. The example of France and other countries which devalued their currencies after the war duly confirms this contention. The index number of French wholesale prices is still at about 400 per cent of the pre-war level. The monetary unit has become smaller and prices will fluctuate in terms of the smaller units. Even though a reaction inevitably follows stabilization, it would only wipe out a fraction of the rise.

It cannot be emphasized sufficiently that devaluation and stabilization will not in themselves solve for ever the world's economic difficulties. On the basis of our present economic system, cyclic crises would inevitably recur, and the chances are that the artificial rise in prices brought about by monetary means will avenge itself by a crisis of great severity. Monetary management and manipulation in themselves are incapable of averting this new crisis. The problem will have to be tackled at its root, and, instead of attacking the symptoms, the responsible statesmen of mankind will have to penetrate to its foundations by organizing production and distribution. It is only through the adoption of planned economy at least on a national scale, and if possible on an international scale, that the recurrence of crises of increased gravity might be prevented. We have several years at our disposal during which a new system could be established. The task will have to be tackled while the trade cycle is on the upward swing. It would be a mistake if the temporary phase of prosperity that will follow this crisis should make the world forget that its chief problem is yet to be solved.

APPENDIX I

MONETARY POLICY OF THE BRITISH EMPIRE

(1) THE OTTAWA AGREEMENT

THE following is extracted from the Ottawa Resolutions regarding Monetary and Financial Questions.

I

(a) A rise throughout the world in the general levels of wholesale prices is in the highest degree desirable. The evil of falling prices must be attacked by Government and individual action in all its causes, whether political, economic, financial or monetary.

(b) For dealing with the problem in its widest aspects the Governments represented at this Conference record their conviction that international action is urgently necessary, and announce their desire to co-operate with other nations in any practicable measures for raising wholesale prices.

(c) The Conference has considered what action

167

can be taken by the nations of the Commonwealth to help towards raising prices.

As regards monetary factors, the Conference recognizes that the central position of the United Kingdom, not only among the countries of the Commonwealth, but in world trade and finance, makes the United Kingdom a main factor in anything that can be done. The Conference, therefore, welcomes the following statement made on behalf of the United Kingdom by the Chancellor of the Exchequer :

" His Majesty's Government desire to see wholesale sterling prices rise. The best condition for this would be a rise in gold prices, and the absence of a rise in gold prices inevitably imposes limitations on what can be done for sterling. A rise in prices cannot be effected by monetary action alone, since various other factors which have combined to bring about the present depression must also be modified or removed before a remedy is assured. His Majesty's Government, nevertheless, recognize that an ample supply of short-term money at low rates may have a valuable influence, and they are confident that the efforts which have successfully brought about the present favourable monetary conditions can and will, unless unforeseen difficulties arise, be continued."

(*d*) The Conference recommends the other countries of the Commonwealth represented here to act in conformity with the line of policy as set out in the statement of the Chancellor of the Exchequer, so far as lies within their power.

In the monetary sphere the primary line of action towards a rise in prices should be the creation and maintenance, within the limits of sound finance, of such conditions as will assist in the revival of enterprise and trade. Among these conditions are low rates of interest and an abundance of short-term money. While regard must be had to the different conditions applying to various types of loans, the rate of interest for all purposes should be kept as low as financial conditions permit. At the same time it is necessary that these favourable monetary conditions be achieved, not by the inflationary creation of additional means of payment to finance public expenditure, but by an orderly monetary policy, safeguarded, if the necessity should arise, by such steps as will restrain and circumscribe the scope of violent speculative movements in commodities or securities.

It must be kept in mind, however, that the success of any such policy will be hampered and might be nullified by the failure to modify or remove important non-monetary obstacles. Of the non-monetary factors which are depressing the level of prices many are of international character and require an international remedy. The nations of the Commonwealth should, nevertheless, take all steps that lie in their power to increase public confidence, especially in the field of business enterprise, and to facilitate trade.

(e) The Conference recognizes the great importance to traders of stability of exchange rates over as wide an area as possible. The complete solution of this problem must await the restoration of conditions for the satisfactory working of an international standard as referred to below. In the meanwhile, and pending such a solution, this Conference has considered the possibility of achieving valuable results in two directions—first by creating an area of stability among countries regulating their currencies in relation to sterling ; and secondly, by avoiding wide day-to-day fluctuations between sterling and gold.

As regards the latter, the Conference has noted with satisfaction that the United Kingdom has already established machinery aimed at preventing wide fluctuations in the gold value of sterling caused by speculative movements. As to the former, the Conference recognizes the value of the countries within the Commonwealth whose currencies are linked to sterling maintaining stability between their exchange rates and looks to a rise in the general level of wholesale prices as the most desirable means for facilitating this result.

II

The Conference recognizes that the ultimate aim of monetary policy should be the restoration of a satisfactory international monetary standard. Such a standard should so function as not merely to maintain stable exchange rates between all countries, but also to ensure the smooth and efficient working of the machinery of international trade and finance.

This postulates international agreement among the great trading nations of the world, and while certain of the States here represented hold very definite views on the question of the most desirable standard, the Conference refrains from making any recommendations on the subject in view of the fact that the question is shortly to be discussed at an international conference. There are, however, several conditions precedent to the re-establishment of any international monetary standard. The most important among them are : a rise in the general level of commodity prices in the various countries to a height more in keeping with the level of costs, including the burden of debt and other fixed and semi-fixed charges ; and an adjustment of the factors political, economic, financial and monetary, which have caused the breakdown of the gold standard in many countries, and which, if not adjusted, would inevitably lead to another breakdown of whatever international standard may be adopted.

It is also in the view of the Conference of the utmost importance to the future working of any international standard that international co-operation should be secured and maintained with a view to avoiding, so far as may be found practicable, wide fluctuations in the, purchasing power of the standard of value.

(2) The London Manifesto

The following is extracted from the manifesto issued by the British Empire delegations at the World Economic Conference.

At the Ottawa Conference the Governments represented declared their view that a rise throughout the world in the general level of wholesale prices was in the highest degree desirable, and stated that they were anxious to co-operate in any practicable measures for raising wholesale prices.

They agreed that a rise in prices could not be

effected by monetary action alone, since various other factors which combined to bring about the present depression must also be modified or removed before a remedy is assured.

It was indicated that international action would be needed to remove the various non-monetary factors which were depressing the level of prices.

In the monetary sphere, the primary line of action towards a rise in prices was stated to be the creation and maintenance within the limits of sound finance of such conditions as would assist in the revival of enterprise, including low rates of interest and an abundance of short-term money. The inflationary creation of additional means of payment to finance public expenditure was deprecated, and an orderly monetary policy was demanded with safeguards to limit the scope of violent speculative movements.

Since then the policy of the British Commonwealth has been directed to raising prices.

The delegations note with satisfaction that this policy has been attended with an encouraging measure of success. For some months, indeed, it had to encounter obstacles arising from the continuance of a downward trend of gold prices, and during that period the results achieved were in the main limited to raising prices in Empire currencies relatively to gold prices. In the last few months the persistent adherence of the United Kingdom to the policy of cheap and plentiful money has been increasingly effective under the more favourable conditions that have been created for the time being by the change of policy of the United States, and by the halt in the fall of gold prices.

Taking the whole period from June 29, 1932, just before the assembly of the Ottawa Conference, a rise in sterling wholesale prices has taken place of 12 per cent, according to the *Economist* index. The rise in the sterling prices of primary products during the same period has been much more substantial, being in the neighbourhood of 20 per cent.

The delegations are of opinion that the views they expressed at Ottawa as to the necessity of a rise in the price level still hold good, and that it is of the greatest importance that this rise which has begun should continue. As to the ultimate level to be aimed at, they do not consider it practicable to state this in precise terms. Any price level would be satisfactory which restores the normal activity of industry and employment, which ensures an economic return to the producer of primary commodities, and which harmonizes the burden of debts and fixed charges with economic capacity.

It is important that the rise in prices should not be carried to such a pitch as to produce an inflated scale of profits and threaten a disturbance of equilibrium in the opposite direction.

The delegations, therefore, consider that the Governments of the British Commonwealth should persist by all means in their power, whether monetary or economic, within the limits of sound finance, in the policy of furthering the rise in wholesale prices until there is evidence that equilibrium has been re-established.

Thereupon they should take whatever measures are possible to stabilize the position thus attained.

With reference to the proposal which has been made from time to time for the expansion of Government programmes of capital outlay, the delegations consider that this is a matter which must be dealt with by each Government in the light of its own experience and of its own conditions.

The Ottawa Conference declared that the ultimate aim of monetary policy must be the restoration of a satisfactory international monetary standard, having in mind not merely stable exchange rates between all countries, but the deliberate management of the international standard in such a manner as to ensure the smooth and efficient working of international trade and finance.

The principal conditions precedent to the re-establishment of any international monetary standard were stated, particularly a rise in the general level of commodity prices in the various countries to a height more in keeping with the level of costs, including the burden of debt and other fixed and semi-fixed charges, and the Conference expressed its sense of the importance of securing and maintaining international co-operation with a view to avoiding, so far as may be found practicable, wide fluctuations in the purchasing power of the standard of value.

The delegations now reaffirm their view that the ultimate aim of monetary policy should be the restoration of a satisfactory international gold standard, under which international co-operation would be secured and maintained with a view to avoiding, so far as may be found practicable, undue fluctuations in the purchasing power of gold.

The problem with which the world is faced is to reconcile the stability of exchange rates with a reasonable measure of stability, not merely in the price level of a particular country, but in world prices. Effective action in this matter must largely depend on international co-operation, and in any further sessions of the World Economic and Monetary Conference this subject must have special prominence.

In the meantime, the delegations recognize the importance of stability of exchange rates between the countries of the Empire in the interests of trade. This objective will be constantly kept in mind in determining their monetary policy, and its achievement will be aided by the pursuit of a common policy of raising price levels.

Inter-Imperial stability of exchange rates is facilitated by the fact that the United Kingdom Government has no commitments to other countries as regards the future management of sterling and retains complete freedom of action in this respect.

The adherence of other countries to a policy on similar lines would make possible the attainment and maintenance of exchange stability over a still wider area.

Among the factors working for the economic recovery of the countries of the Commonwealth, special importance attaches to the decline in the rate of interest on long-term loans.

The delegations note with satisfaction the progress which has been made in that direction as well as in the resumption of overseas lending by

N

the London market. They agree that further advances on these lines will be beneficial as and when they can be made.

The delegations have agreed that they will recommend their Governments to consult with one another from time to time on monetary and economic policy with a view to establishing their common purpose and to the framing of such measures as may conduce towards its achievement.

APPENDIX II

THE ECONOMIC CONFERENCE

THE following is the text of the Report of the Monetary and Financial Commission of the World Economic Conference :

I. REPORT BY H.E. M. GEORGES BONNET
(FRANCE)

1. The Monetary and Financial Commission began work under the Presidency of Governor Cox on June 16. It decided at its first meeting to adopt the Draft Annotated Agenda drawn up by the Preparatory Commission of Experts as the basis of its programme.

With a view to systematic study of its programme, the Commission divided into two Sub-Commissions. The first on " Immediate Measures for Financial Reconstruction ", with H.E. M. G. Jung as President, had the following subjects on its agenda :

Credit Policy ;

Price Levels ;

Limitation of Monetary Fluctuations ;
Exchange Control ;
Indebtedness ;
Resumption of International Lending.

The second Sub-Commission on " Permanent Measures for the Re-establishment of an International Monetary Standard ", with Dr. Kienböck as President, was charged with the study of the following points :

Functions of Central Banks ;
Co-ordination of their Policies ;
Silver ;
Gold Exchange Standard and other Means of economizing Gold ;
Distribution of Monetary Reserves.

All the countries represented at the Conference were entitled to take part in the work of the two Sub-Commissions, and representatives of the Financial Committee of the League of Nations and the President of the Bank for International Settlements were also invited to participate.

Further, each of the two Sub-Commissions entrusted the study of certain special problems and the drawing up of draft resolutions to small sub-committees as circumstances required.

2. A number of meetings were devoted by each of the Sub-Commissions to a detailed exchange of

views on the general aspects of the questions form-
ing their programme as outlined above. This
initial work brought to light the inter-dependence
of the majority of the problems involved, and the
necessity for first settling certain fundamental
questions which might pave the way to the agreements which it was the function of the Sub-Commissions to seek. It was, however, agreed after a
full exchange of views that solutions of these fundamental problems on an international basis were
for the moment impossible, and that in these circumstances it was better to postpone their discussion.
The Sub-Commissions accordingly decided to con-
centrate on those points the discussion of which
was likely to lead to immediate results, and in
agreement with the Bureau of the Conference they
modified their programme accordingly.

3. In these circumstances, they achieved the
results which you will find embodied in the Reports
they have prepared. These Reports have been
adopted by the Monetary and Financial Commission and I, in my turn, have the honour to
submit them to you for your approval.

4. The Sub-Commission I unanimously adopted
the text of a resolution relating to indebtedness
submitted to it by the Drafting Committee set up
for the purpose. The adoption of this resolution

was accompanied by interpretative explanations from the delegations of the Argentine Republic and the Dominican Republic.

The Sub-Commission I brings its Report to a close with the statement that the discussion of the other subjects on the Agenda did not proceed far enough to do more than outline the main problems to be solved. It adds that it will, however, be prepared to resume its task at a later stage.

5. The Sub-Commission II unanimously adopted the following five resolutions :

(*a*) A resolution relating to the return to monetary stability, the adoption of gold as an international monetary standard, its use for monetary requirements and the legal cover of Central Banks.

The Bulgarian delegation made a reservation with regard to this resolution.

(*b*) A resolution relating to the creation of Central Banks.

(*c*) A resolution relating to the need for close and continuous co-operation between Central Banks and to the part which might be played by the Bank for International Settlements in this connection.

(*d*) A resolution relating to the adaptation of

the Central Banks of certain agricultural countries to the special economic conditions of those countries.

The Yugoslav delegation entered a reservation to this resolution.

(e) A resolution relating to silver, the adoption of which was accompanied by explanations from the Mexican delegation and an interpretation by the French delegation.

Sub-Commission II further mentions in its Report the communication made to it by one of its Sub-Committees regarding the general principles of the monetary policy of Central Banks. All the Governments represented on the Sub-Committee approved these principles, except the United States delegation, which considered discussion of the question at this time premature, it being understood that the Federal Reserve Banks would be glad to confer at an opportune time with other Central Banks on questions of this character to the extent that they were compatible with national policies.

With regard to the part of its agenda dealing with the gold exchange standard and other methods of economizing gold, and the distribution of monetary reserves, Sub-Commission II was not able to complete its Report during the present session.

It took note, however, of a recommendation

made to it by the Sub-Committee entrusted with the study of these questions, to the effect that the Bank for International Settlements would examine the problem of the gold exchange standard as soon as possible and would, in particular, consider how far it might be found possible to avoid some of the drawbacks which this system has revealed in the past. The Conference will certainly wish to endorse this recommendation.

6. The Conference will not fail to appreciate the importance of the results already obtained. It is, I think, reasonable to suppose that, when the future work of the Monetary and Financial Commission has led to the conclusion of wider agreements, these agreements will embody the principles which the resolutions adopted record.

Before concluding my report, I should like to draw the attention of the Conference to the extreme importance of the discussions which have taken place at the meetings of your Monetary and Financial Commission and of its various organs of inquiry and which could not be faithfully reflected in the resolutions submitted to you. The questions reserved for further study also gave rise to exhaustive discussions in which all those taking part were inspired by a sense of the grave nature of the task devolving upon this Conference and by a wish to reach solutions which would justify the hopes the whole world has set upon it. If your Commission has not on this occasion solved all the problems submitted to it, it feels sure that a way will soon be found to reconcile views which, differing as regards means, are identical as regards the ultimate aims. On the resumption of the general discussions, which the Bureau will be empowered to arrange for when the time comes, the real value of the substantial work done by your Monetary and Financial Commission at this first session will become fully apparent.

REPORT OF SUB-COMMISSION I : IMMEDIATE MEASURES FOR FINANCIAL RECONSTRUCTION

Chairman : H.E. M. Guido JUNG (Italy)

Following the appointment of the Sub-Commission on Immediate Measures for financial reconstruction by the Monetary and Financial Commission to consider the following questions—credit policy, price levels, limitation of currency fluctuations, exchange controls, problems of indebtedness, resumption of lending—the first meeting of your Sub-Commission was held on June 19 and five public sessions were held between June 19 and 21, in which a general discussion took place on the questions of credit policy and price levels. A draft resolution was submitted by the United Kingdom delegation and a further resolution was proposed by the United States delegation.

Four public sessions followed between June 22 and 27, in which a general discussion took place on the problems of indebtedness. Draft resolutions were submitted by the Hungarian and Roumanian delegations.

On June 27, it was decided to appoint a Sub-Committee to make concrete proposals relating to the procedure to be adopted.

This Sub-Committee met the same day and decided to appoint two Drafting Committees to prepare resolutions, the first on the question of credit policy and the second on the problems of indebtedness.

The first Drafting Committee met on June 28, and discussed a paper submitted by the United Kingdom delegation. However, the working of this Committee was deferred in view of certain events affecting the possibility of reaching, for the time being, full agreement on the terms of resolutions on the subject.

The general policy was reviewed by the Bureau of the Conference at its meeting on July 6, when it requested each Sub-Commission to draw up as soon as possible a list of questions which, in the circumstances, could be usefully studied.

Your Sub-Commission held two public sessions on July 7 in connection with this request, and a proposal of the United Kingdom delegation that all the items on the agenda should be included in the list to be submitted to the Bureau was adopted by 25 votes to 15, with one abstention ; 23 delegations were not present. Three of these subsequently expressed their adherence to the United Kingdom proposal.

On July 11, the Bureau of the Conference decided to recommend that your Sub-Commission should proceed for the time being with the discussion on the problems of indebtedness. This task was confided to the second Drafting Committee appointed on June 27, which held five private meetings between July 12 and 18, and reported through the Chancellor of the Exchequer on July 20 to your Sub-Commission the following resolution, which was unanimously adopted :

1. The service of external debts is in different degrees an important item among the liabilities in the balance of payments of many countries and can only be assured if the debtor country can procure the necessary resources. The facility with which such resources can be procured in

the present and in the future may depend on
the revival of economic activity and credit. It
would be assisted by a return to a reasonable
degree of freedom in the movement of goods
and services and the creditor countries in particular should co-operate to this end. It will
also depend on the economic and financial policy
adopted by the debtor country. In present
conditions a solution of the problem of indebtedness may in certain cases be necessary for the
re-establishment of equilibrium. It should not,
however, be dealt with in such a way as to
impair credit.

2. The conditions in the debtor countries vary
considerably and it is not possible to lay down
a uniform treatment applicable to all cases.
But debtors should make every possible effort
to meet the service of their debts and to fulfil
their contracts. It is indispensable, indeed, for
the restoration of credit that contracts should
be respected in the absence of modifications
agreed between the parties concerned.

3. When arrangements are recognized to be
necessary care should be taken by all concerned
to secure the maintenance of confidence. They
should, therefore, be limited to those cases where
they are unavoidable, be made directly between

debtors and creditors and be based on the debtor's ability to pay. As regards State loans, it is in the interest of the creditors themselves to conclude arrangements of such a nature as will permit the adoption at the same time of a programme of economic and financial restoration by the debtor countries and its effective application.

4. It is desirable that in each of the countries concerned there should exist organizations in a position to represent the several classes of creditors in respect of foreign loans, including, in suitable cases, short as well as long term loans, and that such organizations should maintain such contact with one another as may be necessary to facilitate their proceedings. The Commission therefore recommends to the Governments of these countries that they should encourage the creation of and contact between organizations of this kind where they do not already exist, at such times and in such measure as action can in their view be usefully applied.

5. The question of intergovernmental debts lies entirely outside the field of discussion of this Conference.

The discussion of the other subjects on the agenda did not proceed far enough to do more than outline the main problems to be solved. Your Sub-Commission will however be prepared to resume in order that its task can be completed at a later stage.

REPORT OF SUB-COMMISSION II : PERMANENT MEASURES FOR THE RE-ESTABLISHMENT OF AN INTERNATIONAL MONETARY STANDARD

Chairman : Dr. V. KIENBÖCK (Austria)

1. On June 19, the Monetary and Financial Commission decided to divide its work between two Sub-Commissions. Sub-Commission II, with which this report deals, was set up to consider Permanent Measures for the Re-establishment of an International Monetary Standard. The agenda proposed for the Sub-Commission was :

The Functions of Central Banks ;

The Co-ordination of their Policies ;

Monetary Reserves ;

Silver.

2. All the delegations at the Conference were invited to send representatives to the Sub-Commission. The representatives of the Financial Committee of the League of Nations and the President of the Bank for International Settlements were also invited to co-operate in its work.

Dr. V. Kienböck (Austria) was appointed President of the Sub-Commission.

3. At its first meeting (June 19) the Sub-Commission took as the basis of its discussions a draft resolution submitted by the United States delegation, the second part of a proposal submitted by the Swiss delegation to Sub-Commission I, and the second part of proposals submitted by the Roumanian delegation on behalf of the Bulgarian, Latvian, Polish, Roumanian, Czechoslovak and Yugoslav delegations. It was decided to set up two Sub-Committees, one to deal with the question of silver and the second to deal with the technical monetary problems connected with the working of the gold standard. Senator Pittman presided over the former and Dr. Kienböck, and in his absence Mr. Postmus, over the latter.

4. At its second meeting on June 20, the Sub-Commission unanimously adopted the following resolutions :

I. (*a*) That it is in the interests of all concerned that stability in the international monetary field be attained as quickly as practicable ;

(*b*) That gold should be re-established as the international measure of exchange values, time and parity being for each country to determine.

5. After private discussions and conversations among the delegations primarily concerned, the

Sub-Commission, on July 20, on the recommendation of the Sub-Committee on Silver, unanimously adopted the following draft resolution which was based on a draft submitted by the United States delegation :

Be it resolved to recommend to all the Governments Parties to this Conference

V. (*a*) That an agreement be sought between the chief silver producing countries and those countries which are the largest holders or users of silver, with a view to mitigating fluctuations in the price of silver ; and that the other nations not parties to such agreement should refrain from measures which could appreciably affect the silver market ;

(*b*) That Governments parties to this Conference shall refrain from new legislative measures which would involve further debasement of their silver coinage below a fineness of 800/1000.

(*c*) That they shall substitute silver coins for low value paper currency in so far as the budgetary and local conditions of each country will permit ;

(*d*) That all of the provisions of this Resolution are subject to the following exceptions and limitations :

The requirements of such provisions shall

lapse on April 1, 1934, if the agreement recommended in paragraph (a) does not come into force by that date, and in no case shall extend beyond January 1, 1938 ;

Governments may take any action relative to their silver coinage that they may deem necessary to prevent the flight or destruction of their silver coinage by reason of a rise in the bullion price of the silver content of their coin above the nominal or parity value of such silver coin.

6. The Sub-Committee on Technical Monetary Problems began its work on June 21, with a consideration of monetary gold reserves, taking as the basis of its discussion clauses (c), (d) and (e) of the draft resolution presented by the United States delegation. Mr. Fraser, President of the Bank for International Settlements, was appointed rapporteur.

7. At the fourth meeting of the Sub-Commission held on June 28, the following resolutions were presented :

I. (c) That under modern conditions monetary gold is required not for internal circulation but as a reserve against Central Bank liabilities and primarily to meet external demands for payments caused by some disequilibrium on the foreign account. It is consequently undesirable to put gold coins or gold certificates into internal circulation.

(*d*) That in order to improve the working of a future gold standard greater elasticity should be given to Central Bank legal cover provisions ; for instance, in so far as the system of percentage gold cover is applied a minimum ratio of not more than 25 per cent should be considered as sufficient ; similar elasticity should be achieved by appropriate measures where other systems are applied. However, such changes must not be taken as an excuse for unduly building up a larger superstructure of notes and credits ; in other words the effect of this resolution should be to increase the free reserve of Central Banks and thereby to strengthen their position.

These resolutions were unanimously adopted by the Sub-Commission with an amendment proposed by the Egyptian delegation that the word " minimum " should be inserted before " ratio " in draft resolution (*d*). The Bulgarian delegation while accepting the draft resolution (*c*) made the reservation that in present conditions its Government was unable to use its Central Bank's gold reserves to meet the disequilibrium on the foreign account because such a step would prove seriously prejudicial to public confidence in the note circulation.

The German delegation having proposed to insert the word " temporary " before " disequilibrium " in draft resolution (c), in order to make it clear that the resolution did not favour the use of Central Bank gold reserves to meet a permanent disequilibrium in the balance of payments, withdrew its proposal upon the Rapporteur explaining that the resolution did not mean that Central Banks of countries with a permanent deficit in their balance of accounts would have to be deprived of the whole of the gold in their possession and so compromise the internal note circulation.

8. The Sub-Committee on Technical Monetary Problems resumed consideration of the remaining items of its agenda on June 29, dealing with co-operation among Central Banks. In this connection it took into consideration a proposal by the Roumanian delegation concerning the adaptation of the Central Banks of agricultural countries to the special conditions of those countries.

9. On July 11, the Bureau of the Conference adopted a resolution that—

The Monetary and Financial Sub-Commission II should take up the resolutions, already adopted by its Sub-Committees, on Central Banking co-operation and on the creation of Central Banks in certain countries where they do not now exist, and should pursue, through its Sub-Committees, the examination of the question of silver and any other subject on its agenda which may by general agreement be considered suitable for discussion.

10. In pursuance of the Bureau's resolution, the Sub-Commission met on July 14, and unanimously adopted the three following resolutions :

II. The Conference considers it to be essential, in order to provide an international gold standard with the necessary mechanism for satisfactory working, that independent Central Banks, with the requisite powers and freedom to carry out an appropriate currency and credit policy, should be created in such developed countries as have not at present an adequate Central Banking institution.

III. The Conference wish to reaffirm the declarations of previous conferences with regard to the great utility of close and continuous co-operation between Central Banks. The Bank for International Settlements should play an increasingly important part not only by improving contact, but also as an instrument for common action.

IV. The Sub-Committee has taken note of

the suggestions of the Roumanian delegation
with a view to securing the adaptation of the
Central Banks of certain agricultural countries
to the special economic conditions of these
countries and of the views expressed in the discussion thereof. The Sub-Committee feels that
the local conditions in each country will to a
very large extent determine the solutions to be
adopted in this matter and suggests that if any
countries desire advice on these questions in
view of their technical character they might
appropriately be considered by the international
organizations specially competent to advise on
these matters.

The Yugoslav delegation made a declaration
accepting Resolution IV, at the same time stating
that the legal minimum cover should not be diminished below the percentage recommended by the
Sub-Commission in Resolution I (d).

11. The Sub-Commission held its final meeting
on Monetary Problems on July 20. The following
resolution was communicated to it :

The Sub-Committee approves the annexed
statement of general principles of Central Banks
monetary policy which was laid before it.

(1) The proper functioning of the gold
standard requires in the first place the adoption

by each individual Central Bank of a policy designed to maintain a fundamental equilibrium in the balance of payments of its country. Gold movements which reflect a lack of such an equilibrium constitute therefore an essential factor in determining Central Bank policy.

(2) Gold movements so far as they seem to be of a more permanent character should normally not be prevented from making their influence felt both in the country losing gold and in the country receiving gold.

(3) While gold should be allowed freely to flow out of and into the countries concerned, Central Banks should always be prepared to buy gold at a publicly announced fixed price, expressed in their currency, and to sell gold at a publicly announced fixed price, expressed in their currency, the latter at least when exchange rates reach gold points.

(4) Central Banks should obtain from their markets the fullest possible information concerning the demands that might be made upon their reserves.

(5) Since as already stated under (1) the proper functioning of the gold standard requires in the first place the adoption by each individual Central Bank of a policy designed to

maintain a fundamental equilibrium in the balance of payments of its country, the discretion of each Central Bank in regulating the working of the gold standard in its own country should remain unimpaired. Central Banks should, however, recognize that in addition to their national task they have also to fulfil a task of international character. Their aim should be to co-ordinate the policy pursued in the various centres in order to contribute towards the satisfactory working of the international gold standard system.

Moreover, they should endeavour to adapt their measures of credit regulation, as far as their domestic position permits, to any tendency towards an undue change in the state of general business activity. An expansion of general business activity of a kind which clearly cannot be permanently maintained, should lead Central Banks to introduce a bias towards credit restriction into the credit policy which they think fit to adopt, having regard to internal conditions in their own countries. On the other hand, an undue decline in general business activity in the world at large should lead them to introduce a bias towards relaxation.

In pursuing such a policy the Central Banks

will have done what is in their power to reduce fluctuations in business activity and thereby also undue fluctuations in the purchasing power of gold.

(6) With a view to arriving at an agreed interpretation of the data revealing the tendency of developments in general business activity, and at an agreed policy, Central Banks should consult together continuously, each Central Bank in case of difference of opinion, acting on its own judgment of the situation. The Bank for International Settlements constitutes an essential agency for Central Bank action designed to harmonize conflicting views and for joint consultation. This instrument should continue to be employed, as far as possible, for the realization of the principles set forth in the present note. It should continuously examine the application of the principles of the working of the gold standard and study such modifications thereof as experience may prove desirable.

Agreement on the resolution was reached by all governments represented at the Sub-Committee on Technical Monetary Problems, except that of the United States of America, which considered discussion of the question at this time premature, it being understood that the Federal Reserve Banks would be glad to confer at an opportune time with other Central Banks on questions of this character to the extent that they are compatible with national policies.

The Sub-Commission further took note of a report from the Sub-Committee on Technical Monetary Problems concerning the remaining subjects on its agenda, including a draft resolution submitted by the Irish Free State delegation. The report was as follows :

The Committee has not been able during the present session to complete its report on the section of the Annotated Agenda dealing with the gold exchange standard, with other methods of economizing gold and with distribution of monetary reserves.

As regards the gold exchange standard, the Committee recommends that the Bank for International Settlements should as soon as possible proceed to a study of the question and particularly that it should examine to what extent it will prove possible to avoid certain of the defects which this system has revealed in the past.

12. The Sub-Commission was asked to clarify the permanent principles of monetary policy that ought to be pursued in future. It is satisfactory

to note that it has achieved a measure of success in this task since it has proved possible to reach full agreement on certain important problems. This may be seen from the text of resolutions approved. The same unanimity was evident also in regard to the necessity of central bank co-operation. Finally it should be stated that the important task which the Bank for International Settlements must discharge in the future was fully recognized.

APPENDIX III

THE ROOSEVELT NOTE

THE following is the text of the proposed joint declaration which was offered to the United States on July 1, 1933 for her signature :

I. The undersigned Governments agree that

(a) It is in the interests of all concerned that stability in the international monetary field be attained as quickly as practicable ;

(b) That gold should be re-established as the international measure of exchange value, it being recognized that the parity and time at which each of the countries now off gold could undertake to stabilize must be decided by the respective governments concerned.

II. The signatory Governments whose currencies are on the gold standard reassert that it is their determination to maintain the free working of that standard at the existing gold parities within the framework of their respective monetary laws.

III. The signatory Governments whose currencies are not on the gold standard, without in any way prejudicing their own future ratios to gold, take note of the above declaration and recognize its importance. They re-affirm that the ultimate objective of their monetary policy is to restore, under proper conditions, an international monetary standard based on gold.

IV. Each of the signatory Governments whose currencies are not on the gold standard undertakes to adopt the measures which it may deem most appropriate to limit exchange speculation, and each of the other signatory Governments undertakes to co-operate to the same end.

V. Each of the undersigned Governments agrees to ask its central bank to co-operate with the central banks of the other signatory Governments in limiting speculation in the exchanges and, when the time comes, in re-establishing a general international gold standard.

VI. The present declaration is open to signature by other Governments, whether their currencies are on the gold standard or not.

The following is the text of President Roosevelt's answer to above proposals, and read by Mr. Cordell Hull, United States Secretary of State, at the Economic Conference on July 4, 1933 :

Mr. Cordell Hull, in an introduction to the

statement, says : " I have this morning received the following communication from the President of the United States setting forth the position of our Government relative to suggested international currency measure proposals.

" I am making this public in my capacity of Secretary of State and not as chairman of the American delegation, since the delegation has at no time had jurisdiction of this subject, which is purely a Treasury matter."

President Roosevelt's statement reads as follows :

" I would regard it as a catastrophe amounting to world tragedy if the great Conference of nations called to bring about a more real and permanent financial stability and a greater prosperity to the masses of all nations should, in advance of any serious efforts to consider these broader problems, allow itself to be diverted by the proposal of a purely financial and temporary experiment affecting the monetary exchange of a few nations only.

" Such action, such diversion, shows a singular lack of proportion and a failure to remember the larger purposes for which the Economic Conference originally was called together.

" I do not relish the thought that insistence on such action should be made an excuse for the continuance of the basic economic errors that underlie so much of the present world-wide depression.

" The world will not long be lulled by the specious fallacy of achieving a temporary, and probably an artificial, stability in foreign exchange on the part of a few large countries only. The sound internal economic system of a nation is a greater factor in its well-being than the price of its currency in changing terms of the currencies of other nations.

" It is for this reason that reduced cost of Government, adequate Government income and ability to service Government debts are all so important to ultimate stability.

" So, too, old fetishes of so-called international bankers are being replaced by efforts to plan national currencies with the objective of giving to those currencies a continuing purchasing power which does not greatly vary in terms of the commodities and need of modern civilization.

" Let me be frank in saying that the United States seeks the kind of a dollar which a generation hence will have the same purchasing and debt-paying power as the dollar value we hope to attain in the near future.

" That objective means more to the good of other nations than a fixed ratio for a month or two in terms of the pound or franc.

" Our broad purpose is the permanent stabilization of every nation's currency. Gold or gold and
silver can well continue to be a metallic reserve
behind currencies, but this is not the time to dissipate
gold reserves.

" When the world works out concerted policies
in the majority of nations to produce balanced
Budgets and living within their means, then we
can properly discuss a better distribution of the
world's gold and silver supply to act as a reserve
base of national currencies.

" Restoration of world trade is an important
partner both in the means and in the result. Here,
also, temporary exchange fixing is not the true
answer. We must rather mitigate existing embar-
goes to make easier the exchange of products which
one nation has and the other has not.

" The Conference was called to better and perhaps
to cure fundamental economic ills. It must not
be diverted from that effort."